What Others Are Saying

"Dorcas Smucker's knack for storytelling and her way of gleaning wise insights from daily experiences always touches my spirit—both uplifting and challenging me to gain more from my own life. No matter how many times I read her tales, they're always fresh and enjoyable. I cannot recommend them highly enough."

—Mary Hake, *past president of Oregon Christian Writers*

"That Dorcas Smucker has found an impassioned following in a time and place that often clash with her farm-rooted values is a glowing testament to what may be her greatest attribute as a writer: her ability, with words, to transcend politics, geography, and lifestyles and connect with something far more important. Her readers' hearts."

"Smucker is unpretentious, genuine and sneakily funny. She is that rare writer who eschews the cultural flow, a true nonconformist in a world of wanna-bes. A quiet spirt who dares to teach us lessons we didn't realize we needed until they've already settled deeply into our souls."

—Bob Welch, *author and inspirational speaker*

"Dorcas Smucker's "Letter from Harrisburg" has been delivering thoughtful essays and a unique perspective on family life to Register-Guard readers for more than 14 years now. Her smooth and heartfelt writing style captures life lessons with humor and grace, all documented from a century-old farmhouse and through the voices of her Mennonite minister husband, Paul, and their six children."

—Mark Baker, *senior writer at The Register-Guard*

Also by Dorcas Smucker

Ordinary Days
Upstairs the Peasants are Revolting
Downstairs the Queen is Knitting

Published by Good Books
Intercourse, Pennsylvania

Tea and Trouble Brewing

Published by Muddy Creek Press
Harrisburg, Oregon

Footprints
on the
Ceiling

Dorcas Smucker

Muddy Creek Press
Harrisburg, Oregon

Published by Muddy Creek Press
Harrisburg, Oregon

For ordering information or to contact Dorcas:
dorcassmucker@gmail.com
or
31148 Substation Drive
Harrisburg, OR 97446

Social media:
Facebook: http://www.facebook.com/Smucker.Dorcas
Blog: "Life in the Shoe" www.dorcassmucker.blogspot.com

Book design by Tom Penix
tompenix@gmail.com

Back cover photo of author by Kristiann Photography

ISBN: 978-0-9883329-4-2
Printed in Canada

Unless otherwise noted, all Scripture quotations are taken from THE HOLY BIBLE, NEW INTERNATIONAL VERSION®, NIV® Copyright © 1973, 1978, 1984, 2011 by Biblica, Inc.® Used by permission. All rights reserved worldwide.

Scripture labeled KJV is from the Holy Bible, King James Version.

The quote on Page 181 is from "O Holy Night"("Cantique de Noël" by Placide Cappeau) translated from French to English by John Sullivan Dwight.

All the essays in this book originally appeared in *The Register-Guard*, Eugene, Oregon.

While this book is non-fiction, a few names and identifying details have been changed for the sake of privacy.

Acknowledgments

Thank you to *The Register-Guard* newspaper in Eugene, Oregon, for carrying my "Letter from Harrisburg" column for the past fourteen years; to my understanding editor, Mark Baker; and to all the subscribers who took the time to look up the "Letter from Harrisburg" and read it.

Special thanks to my family for all the love, the stories, and the amused tolerance on "Mom meeting her deadline" day. Thank you for letting me write about you, and for keeping the prices reasonable when you weren't sure if you should let me.

Dedication

To Ben,
You loved LEGOS® and numbers and atlases.
You were a diver and Captain Haddock and
Jason Fife the quarterback.
And it was easy to make you laugh.
May you always build and multiply.
May you be an adventurer in far places.
And may you always find laughter again.

Contents

3.
Our Forebears: Black Church Shoes and Four-Buckle Overshoes

4.
Travel: Steps on Faraway Soil

5.
Reflecting: Resting My Feet

Introduction
How We Began: The First Footprint

I was the sort of girl that guys looked through instead of at.

This is not an easy thing: to have your big brother tell your sister that all his friends couldn't wait until she was old enough to date.

And me? Oh. Well, my name didn't really come up.

I coped by throwing my energies into schoolwork and pretending that I was above such fluffy things as romance. I was going to be a doctor or a linguist. I would consider marriage at maybe age thirty-five.

Girls who married young and had babies were throwing their lives away. So dumb.

I did not consult God about my plans, even though I was a Christian in a church that was nearly Amish.

My dad thought I should teach at church schools for a few years before I went to college. Amish and Mennonite schools don't require teachers to have a teaching degree. First, I taught for a year at a church school sixty miles from my home in Minnesota.

I took a few weeks off in the middle of the year and went to a short-term Bible school. There I got my first taste of the Yoder Curse. This is an odd phenomena that has so steadily dogged my sisters and me, and even our daughters and nieces, that we gave it a name. Thanks to my mom, it is embedded in our souls to be nice to the outcasts. So we chat up the greasy-haired guy with acne and high-water pants, and we are kind to the awkward, stammering guy in a roomful of cool. Then these guys fall in love with us because finally, finally, a girl has been kind to them.

So the Yoder Curse hit me at Bible school. "I did not *mean* it that way," I pleaded. "I was just being *kind.*"

Meanwhile, the cool guys who were funny and intellectual and cute looked right past me at the cute, sashaying Pennsylvania girls who had that mysterious something I did not possess.

I left Bible school as cynical about romance as ever, even as longings for romance simmered quietly in my soul.

An older student from Oregon happened to be there that year, and he also happened to be on the board of a Mennonite school. After Bible school, he contacted me and asked if I would consider teaching in Oregon.

I said yes.

In Oregon, I lived with a welcoming Mennonite family, who modeled healthy marriage and family life in a way I had never seen before. They also mentored me in ways I desperately needed.

Among my students was fiery little Rosie Smucker in the fourth grade. Gradually, I got to know her family, especially her sister Barb. The Smuckers were different from anyone I had ever known—outspoken, curious, and utterly oblivious to what anyone thought of them, which was so different from me that I was endlessly intrigued. Barb and I became good friends.

Their older brother Paul taught at a school two hours away. He came home on weekends sometimes and attended church and youth-group activities. I was completely smitten. He was tall and blond and smart, with the family trait of calm confidence that was not arrogance or bravado.

He looked past me too.

I stayed in Oregon over the summer after my first year of teaching there, and I'd concoct excuses to spend time with Barb at her house, hoping to see Paul. But he worked nights and somehow was never around when I was. It was desperately frustrating.

This was when I finally began to seek the Lord, realizing that my conniving might not be His design for me.

But the summer was almost over, and then Paul would go away again and I would hardly ever see him! And what if God never did anything?

One night I knelt by my bed for one of those Jacob-like wrestlings with God. Could I trust Him with this or not? I was tired of scheming. But I also wanted Paul in my life really badly, and God hadn't made it happen.

A poster above my bed said, "Sleep in peace. God is awake."

It spoke to me of trust. "OK," I said, "I am done with scheming. I am not going to pursue him. I will not go to Barb's unless she invites me. I will not connive to spend time with Paul."

Then I slept in peace.

One evening soon after, Barb called and suggested we go on a walk. I said yes, happy that this was her idea and, since it wasn't at their home, I would be keeping my promise and not chasing Paul.

As we walked down the road, Barb said, "Let's go to our warehouse." So we walked down the dusty lane in the evening light.

We went inside the cavernous warehouse, and there was Paul, sacking seed under a big funnel-like hopper. He looked at us and smiled. He looked dusty and handsome.

Barb showed me around and then she showed me that on the ceiling just above the hopper there were painted initials of bygone seedsackers. There was even a footprint.

I said I thought the footprint was very clever.

Barb wondered if I would like my footprint up there.

I said yes.

She told Paul to go into the office until this operation was completed, and then she handed me the inky blacking-brush used for stenciling bags. I took off my sandals and sat on a pallet on the forklift. Barb started the forklift and hoisted me up, and I inked my foot and printed it on the ceiling and put my initials beside it.

I knew this was not the sashaying charm that attracted guys, but I didn't care so much about that at the moment. I just wanted to have fun.

We let Paul out of the office and he went back to sacking.

Later I found out that the footprint on the ceiling was the jolt that made him look at me instead of past me. *She is not like other girls,* he thought.

That October he called me and asked if I'd consider a date with him on the thirtieth. In the wild nervousness of the moment, I said the most idiotic thing, which was "Well, if I'm not out trick-or-treating."

Then I said, "Yes."

And, later, since he astonishingly kept asking, I said more yeses.

Today, we own that warehouse, and that footprint is still on the ceiling. Paul is still full of calm confidence. He still looks at me and not past me. I have changed my ideas about romance. I have learned a lot about trusting God.

We eventually had six children, an old farmhouse that's been in the family for a hundred years, busy lives, and lots of responsibility. The footprint on the ceiling led to many moments when life felt upside down and a bit crazy, many footsteps on the kitchen ceiling above me as children upstairs vied for the bathroom on school mornings, many steps outward to adventures close by and far away, many wandering journeys of the soul.

Our family's adventures found their way into a column in the Eugene, Oregon, *Register-Guard*, and then into five books, including this one. The stories do not appear in chronological order and can be perused at random, preferably with a cup of tea.

I hope they will make you think of all the paths your life has taken and all the stories you have to tell.

I have no idea what steps and journeys are in our future, but, whatever happens, I hope I will always say yes to Paul.

And to God.

1.

Children:

Flip Flops
and Basketball Shoes

Dots on the Ceiling

School is a good thing, but Paul and I also appreciate the learning that comes with orange spots on the ceiling and apple crisp and Grandma copying e-mails.

You don't have to be in our house long to catch on that education is important. After a summer of fragmented schedules, suddenly the alarm clocks ring at 6:45 a.m. The pancakes are on the plates by 7:15, shoulders bump as sandwiches assemble on the counter, and, soon after 8:00 a.m., five of the six of us are off to school—a teacher and four students, some to our church school and others to a community college.

In the evenings, we jostle for time on the computer, and the task bar at the bottom features Internet searches on the density of water, laborious essays from Steven's Bible class on "How to Let Your Light Shine," and Ben's incomprehensible calculus assignments. "Don't X out of that!" each child tells the next when they switch turns.

Yes, we value education, but even more we value learning that applies to life. Or wisdom, as the Bible calls it, which has a higher purpose than merely knowledge for its own sake. Wisdom integrates not only complicated chemistry formulas but communicating with your sister and caring for body and mind and spirit. It means figuring out what your talents are, recognizing they are gifts from God, and using them to help others.

Somehow, we hope our children also catch the awe of how much information is out there to discover, the humility of knowing how much they don't know, and the joy of lifelong learning.

The frozen can of soda didn't start off as a scientific experiment, sixteen-year-old Steven says. It was just a bright idea.

It happened in the middle of harvest, on a typical day when my husband, Paul, practically lived at our grass-seed warehouse and the two seed-sacking teenage boys met each other coming and going as they slogged through a dusty, daily treadmill of working, eating and sleeping.

I was gone most of that August day, speaking to a gathering of cheerful Methodist women at a church on the coast.

That evening, I relaxed by sitting at the kitchen counter and drinking hot chocolate.

I don't know why I glanced up, but immediately something odd caught my eye.

The ceiling above me was decorated with hundreds of shiny, little orange dots.

Naturally, I inquired about this.

"What's so weird about little orange flecks on the ceiling?" Steven said, providing the first clue that he was somehow involved.

It turned out that while hefting fifty-pound sacks in the heat that afternoon, Steven had decided that the cold orange pop he would soon get out of the old refrigerator by the office would be so much more refreshing if it were frozen solid, or at least slushy. So he put it in the freezer compartment of the fridge.

At 3:00 p.m. when his shift ended, he shook the can and it still wasn't frozen, so he took it home, put it in the freezer in the kitchen, and took a nap.

When he got up, he checked the can again and—yes! It felt good and hard. He decided to get a "sharp cutter thing" out of the desk drawer, slice around the center of the can, and slide the icy treat into a bowl.

However, when he stabbed the side of the can, he told us with a shrug, "It exploded."

His sister, Emily, helped him scrub droplets of orange soda from the counters, the cupboards, the refrigerator, the floor, the dishwasher, and many other places where one normally doesn't find orange dots.

But they forgot to check the ceiling. So Steven climbed on a stool and scrubbed the north half of the ceiling plus the light fixture.

"Did you learn anything?" my husband asked him, the standard question after the wounds are bandaged, the broken items replaced, or the mess wiped up.

"Um, yeah," Steven said. "Apparently carbon doesn't freeze very well."

He meant carbon dioxide, of course, but we didn't correct him. The important and delightful thing was that he had hypothesized, experimented, and observed, remembered a few facts from science class, and drawn conclusions. He also took responsibility for the mess it made, and, even though he finds it difficult to explain such things coherently, assembled the words to tell us exactly what had happened. And, in answer to his dad's question, yes, he had definitely learned something.

He was wiser than before.

Twelve-year-old Jenny, in contrast to Steven, whips through anything academic but gets frustrated when working with food.

Education in daily life skills is just as important as academics, we believe, because the more things you can do for yourself, such as baking, giving haircuts, or fixing a car, the more self-reliant you'll be and the less often you have to hire someone else to do it for you.

So I told Jenny she was going to learn to make apple crisp

just like my mom taught me. She griped about this idea and continued muttering all through choosing the apples and washing them and ramming them on the peeler prongs.

She complained that the apple cores were off-center and that the peeler wouldn't peel, and waited impatiently while I took it apart and put it back together. Then she sighed because I didn't have the recipe written down and just told her each step as my mom used to tell me. She got frustrated because the butter and brown sugar and oatmeal stuck to the fork when she tried to mix them. She didn't start to smile until I told her she could use her fingers instead, and, digging in, she discovered this was fun after all. Finally, she sprinkled the mixture on top of the apples, slid the large pan into the oven, and forty-five minutes later seemed amazed at the browned deliciousness she had just created.

Two or three more repetitions of this, I'm guessing, and Jenny will own that skill for the rest of her life—an intuitive knowledge of this many apples, this much sugar if they're still green, that much crumbly stuff on top. And she will find herself enjoying the process.

One result of wisdom is that you don't keep it to yourself, which is why I sat in my mother-in-law's tidy office a few weeks ago and showed her how to take each of the family e-mails that had come in that week and combine them into "The Smucker Circle Letter," one long e-mail she could send out to everyone, so named because of the old tradition of letters mailed from one family member to the next with contributions from everyone.

"Click on e-mail," she wrote carefully on a paper.

"OK," I said, "Now you click the right-hand button on the mouse. This one."

"Right click on mouse," she repeated, writing.

"Now, 'Select All.'"

She read and followed the directions ten times over until all the e-mails were collected into one. I told my family about this at suppertime, and Emily exclaimed, "What? I showed her that exact process several months ago. She must have forgotten."

"Maybe so," I said, "But I know what it's like to have you guys help me with computer stuff, so I don't mind helping her. And look at her, in her seventies and determined to learn something new."

I hope they found that impressive.

The morning rush to get off to school will no doubt continue for years. More importantly, next month one of the computer-wise people in this house will likely be called down to Grandma's again to help with the circle letter. The bucket of Gravenstein apples will turn into more cobblers and crisps. And, now and then, when I again find a sticky orange dot on the underside of a shelf in the kitchen or the middle of an old grocery list, I will smile, because it means my children are on their way to a lifetime of learning and discovery and wisdom.

Ignoring the Script

The holidays bring out the director in me. Our home is the setting, my family the characters, and I imagine scenes and dialogues and delightful endings, deluding myself into thinking that everyone will follow my enchanting script.

It ought to begin like this, I think. *That is what the characters ought to do and say, and this is how it should all turn out.*

All six children would be home for Christmas, and, months in advance, I was giddy with anticipation. The house would be clean and decorated, I decided, with dozens of cookies stashed in Tupperware containers and carefully selected gifts arranged in the living room.

Best of all would be the endless family camaraderie. Of course, we would all sit together at church on Christmas morning. Laughter and bonhomie and witty conversation would flow around the dinner table. Late at night, I would hear the murmurs of young adults upstairs, pouring out their lives and secrets to caring siblings.

Someday, maybe, I'll catch on that characters in my life have their own ideas and events never go quite as I plan.

I was the first to veer from the script, succumbing on the first of December to a cold that settled in my asthmatic lungs, turned to bronchitis, and left me coughing and tired for weeks. So the cookies never got baked, the presents ended up being last-minute and makeshift, and the only decorations were what twelve-year-old Jenny draped around the living room.

The kids came home, but, as Christmas approached, they

never seemed to have the cozy times I had envisioned, scattering instead to work or shopping or coffee with friends. One evening I found the girls upstairs, each alone in a bedroom, each absorbed in her laptop computer.

This was not how I had decided things ought to be.

Granted, one little scripted scene did come true: The kids indulged me, and we all sat together for the Christmas morning service. It was wonderful—all these beautiful young people in a long row.

Sadly, the perfect scene stopped with that detail. Since we had straggled in one by one, the woman who innocently sat on the west end of the pew before most of us got there ended up getting squished. The sermon went overtime, the boys whispered, and Jenny squirmed past a long line of knees to sit by her "cool" brother, Matt, instead of her dad.

It's not only moms who try to mold real life into a fairy-tale fantasy, because when our daughter Emily got the kitty on Christmas Eve, I'm convinced she was trying to script the perfect moment.

A student at Linn-Benton Community College near Albany, Emily spent months practicing for their production of *A Christmas Carol,* Charles Dickens's story of the miserly Ebenezer Scrooge, who works his clerk, Bob Cratchit, half to death and who is eventually reformed to warmth and generosity and merriment by the visits of three ghosts.

The most minor details were endlessly rehearsed, and the story seemed to seep into Emily's bones. "The goose! The goose!" she exclaimed, like a grateful Cratchit when she saw the Christmas turkey in the freezer. On crisp December mornings she got up and quoted dramatically, "Foggier yet, and colder; piercing, searching, biting cold."

On Christmas Eve, Emily finished her shift at work and stopped at Fred Meyer. In front of the store, a father and daughter stood by a box with a sign that said, "Free Christmas kittens."

What a perfect scene, and Emily knew how it was supposed to turn out. She chose a gray kitten, named it Ebenezer, and laughed indulgently when it turned on her windshield wipers as she drove home.

"I knew we always had room in our home for one more cat," she explained dreamily as though we were such a loving family, like the Cratchits, always full of welcome and good cheer.

Unfortunately, I couldn't play my part. "No. Outside," I insisted. "You have no idea if that cat has lice or fleas or something just as bad."

So Ebenezer went on the porch with the other cats, supplied with food, water, and a rug-lined box. He would be fine, I was sure, convincing myself that I wasn't completely spoiling the heartwarming "Kitten on Christmas Eve" drama.

As it turned out, the kitten didn't need anyone's help to completely ruin the story. He started yowling and kept it up just outside the door all through our traditional Christmas Eve meal, a Kenyan meal of ugali and fresh pineapple and stir-fried kale to celebrate our son, Steven, coming home to us from his native Kenya on Christmas Eve seven years ago.

Ebenezer screeched on Christmas Day as well, through gifts and a big turkey dinner and table games in the evening. Even the loving Cratchits would have run out of warm feelings, I was sure, and a few Smuckers were turning to outright hostility.

While the bad news is that life is not a college drama and it refuses to follow my script, the good news is that life writes its own script, inserting all kinds of priceless moments I would never have thought of including, and it finds ways to turn out all right in the end.

On the way to church, the conversation in the car suddenly turned to stories of Steven at the orphanage, how cute he was, and why we decided to adopt him. We talked about the time he mixed yellow and blue paint and hollered joyfully, "Iss gdeen!"

"What would life be like if we didn't have Steven?" someone said.

"Boring," both Amy and I said. Steven looked embarrassed but pleased.

A priceless and precious moment, and I hadn't planned it at all.

Less cozy but amusing was the exchange between two brothers during the Christmas service. Steven took notes on the sermon for his Bible class at school. He wrote down the sermon title then whispered to Matt, "What's the date today?"

"Dude, what is it?" Matt whispered back.

Steven couldn't remember. Matt refused to tell him. He claimed it took two minutes and thirty-eight seconds for Steven to figure out what the date was.

By the time we all went to the coast overnight a few days after Christmas, I had given up on trying to direct my independent bunch into my ideas of perfect family times.

So, of course, things happened of their own accord—the guys around the table hollering over a Settlers of Catan game and the girls all laughing at a sweet, old movie from the seventies, no laptop open anywhere.

The older kids gave Ben advice about Bible school. Matt installed a program on my computer. Paul pulled in to a Dutch Brothers stand and ordered fancy coffees for the rest of us for the first time in his life. We all enjoyed the hot tub, even Paul and me early one morning—a sight Jenny later described as "disturbing."

Steven thought she was silly. "I guess they're married," he said.

We came home, and the kitty kept yowling. Emily had abandoned all responsibility, and I had no idea what to do. One day I shopped at a discount grocery store and found a little bottle labeled CONTENT-EZE, with this description: "A Nutritional Supplement Which Supports Feeling Of Contentment In Your Cats."

I bought it, knowing it wouldn't do any good but thinking I ought to give it a try.

Jenny and I fixed a dish of leftover tetrazzini, gently squirted a teaspoon of CONTENT-EZE on top, and fed it to Ebenezer, who, to our astonishment, quit yowling.

Everyone hugged everyone else when we all parted ways again. Matt drove back to Corvallis, Ben flew away for three months of Bible school, Amy returned to her volunteer work in Jamaica, and the rest of us slowly adjusted to normal life.

Smiling, I think back to all the quirky, special, funny moments that appeared with no assistance from me, no manipulation from my too-eager motherly fingers.

Maybe someday I'll learn that the script isn't mine to write and the play isn't mine to direct. Life and my family are meant to follow their own paths. The best moments are ad-libbed and unexpected, the ending ultimately more satisfying than my artificial notions of how it all ought to be.

Delightful Differences

I hauled the suitcase to the bedroom upstairs and turned to our guest, twelve-year-old Jenny's friend and second cousin, Dawnisha, better known as Dolly.

"You can choose," I said. "A mattress on the floor, the hide-a-bed, or the top bunk of the loft bed."

"The top bunk, please," Dolly said promptly.

I looked at her tiny frame and shortened arms. Oh, dear, maybe I shouldn't have offered.

"Can you climb up there OK?" I asked.

"Oh, yeah," she scoffed. "As long as I don't wear my back brace."

That's right. She has scoliosis too.

She began unpacking, scattering pajamas and dress-up clothes in a semi-circle on the floor. Jenny picked up a techy-looking white object about four inches long.

"Is this an MP3 player?"

Dolly laughed. "No! That's my hearing aid case!"

Downstairs, Dolly rummaged through the Tupperware in the corner cupboard. "Auntie Dorcas, do you have a minis-cule container on hand? I need it for my vitamins."

Oh, yes. Food allergies. I had forgotten that as well. But—"miniscule"?

I was in for an interesting weekend.

They were born a month apart, these two. First, Jenny, robust and red-haired and the youngest of five. Then my husband's cousin and his wife had Dawnisha, a tiny, fragile first-born, with only a three-fingered stub at her right shoulder

26

and a somewhat longer arm on the left.

The girls had much in common as they grew older. Well-loved, talkative, creative, and a bit precocious, they sang together in a children's choir and canoed down the creek together and jumped on the trampoline and went to the state fair with Dolly's family.

But having Dolly pop in and out of the house on summer afternoons was not like having her here for an entire weekend.

She is, I found, a combination of normal and gifted, of whole and handicapped, of stunted growth and oversized imagination.

I confess to never feeling quite sure about how to behave toward people who stand out because of their appearance, convinced that whether I stare or ignore, talk or keep quiet, it's the wrong response. I admit, this seems a bit odd, seeing as how I stand out in my Mennonite garb.

A severely shy young friend of mine recently posted on Facebook that he had, that day, overcome his impediment enough to look at someone in a wheelchair and say hi. It seemed to me that the visible disability gave him the courage to briefly overcome his own less-obvious handicap.

A rapid online discussion followed. Some felt it was inappropriate to single out a disabled person as somehow safer. Handicapped people should be treated just like you would treat anyone else, they said, and to even ask the question, "How should I treat a handicapped person?" was in itself an insult.

I could see their point. As a Mennonite woman, I don't mind curiosity, but I dislike both reverence and mockery.

"Just like anyone else," works for me, and if the lady beside me at the produce stand casually asks me if and how I cook acorn squash, without seeming to notice any difference between us, I feel strangely affirmed as normal.

It wasn't hard to treat Dolly as I would any twelve-year-old guest. I indulged her love for my gluten-free cereal-and-peanut-butter bars and acted sympathetic, while chuckling inside, when she talked about symptoms of teenage hormones, prefaced by a nervous, "Are there any boys around?"

But sometimes there was simply no getting around the differences. A long-limbed, athletic girl like Jenny is different from one whose arms are like radio antennae that forgot to telescope all the way out.

When the zipper stuck on her jacket, Dolly simply didn't have the leverage to fix it. Nor could she open the container of snack bars by herself.

Fortunately, Dolly herself taught me how she ought to be treated.

When she wanted a drink, I pointed to the right cupboard then realized the glasses were up too high, so I set a step stool in place for her. I turned to work on something else and soon realized that even the step stool wasn't high enough when Dolly said, "Is it OK if I kneel on the counter?"

Should I have simply fetched her drink myself? I wondered.

Dolly answered my unspoken question, "Just so you know, you don't have to do things for me, even if it takes me a lot longer than you."

I was glad to know that.

Children make things less complicated than adults, and I took cues from Jenny as well. On a sunny Saturday afternoon, the two girls crossed the road and played in the deep ditch and among the oak trees on the other side.

Eventually, they decided to dig steps into the dirt to make it easier to go up and down the ditch.

So Dolly stood at the top, her little arms wrapped around a large, red shovel, and there she prodded and pushed and tugged in what seemed to me a pitiful, useless effort.

At the bottom, Jenny pushed dirt aside with her hands, oblivious to Dolly's slow progress. I checked on them once or twice, and both seemed delighted with their project, the mud on their knees, and each other.

But I wondered why in the world Jenny didn't see how Dolly was struggling with that shovel. I swallowed my motherly urges to rush in and direct them, sensing that it was best to take my cues from Jenny. If the girls were happy, I should probably stay out of it.

They came in a long time later, glowing and muddy, totally satisfied with their afternoon's work. I was the only one who had stressed about their arrangement; that was obvious.

"What's the hardest thing?" I asked Dolly that evening, meaning: What normal task did she find most difficult?

She misunderstood. "When I see other kids playing sports."

I considered saying, "Well, I can relate to that."

But I knew that, in reality, I couldn't. Not at all.

So young, so many losses, I thought.

And yet, in other ways, she had so much, such as insights into character. She told me how it works with men like her dad and my husband.

"It's like, with Smucker men, if you keep asking, they dig in their heels. You ask one time, and then it's quiet, and then after a while you say, 'Uh, did you hear me?' and they're like, 'I'm thinking.'"

So young, so wise, so hilariously observant, I thought.

She changed into pajama bottoms and a tank top for the night. I asked which joints of hers correlated with my wrists and elbows. She demonstrated, from shoulders to fingers, showing me which bones were missing, which joints moved, and which didn't.

"And this here is like an elbow, except it's fused," she said, pointing to her left arm. "I'm so glad it's fused in a bend. If it were fused straight, I couldn't comb my hair, or eat! Thank God He made me this way!"

And, then, just like Jenny or any normal twelve-year-old girl, that thought triggered another and she rattled down a different track.

"Do you think that's taking the Lord's name in vain to just say, 'Thank God?' I mean, it's not like I'm kneeling down and praying and, 'Oh, thank You, dear God.' It's like, an expression, you know? 'Thank God this and this!'"

I told her I'm sure it's all about how you mean it in your heart.

Then she and Jenny galloped on in seemingly endless chatter about pajamas and dreams and library books and cats and cute clothes and brothers and making stuff. *She really is just like any other girl,* I thought. Except when she's a lot more so.

Or, as Dolly herself put it, with a delighted grin, "Capable but humble, that's me!"

On Not Getting My Way

I doubt that many Mennonite families are seen wandering around the old brick buildings at the Washington Navy Yard along the Anacostia River near the US Capitol in Washington, DC.

But there we were, long skirts flapping in the breeze, gloved and scarved in the winter chill, wandering past old barracks and heavy, black cannon barrels and a sloping track where ships were once hauled out of the Potomac with an enormous winch.

Our twenty-six-year-old son, Matt, led the way, first flashing his pass to get us through the gate, then proudly showing us the only other Oregon license plate in the parking lot, the outside of the building where he works, the white mansion where the chief of naval operations lives, and the old battleship from Vietnam days.

Then he took us into the Navy museum, where tourists can examine maritime military history and the glorification of long-ago battles and equipment.

Shedding coats and gloves, we wandered around the displays: a copper peg made by Paul Revere himself, taken from a dismantled sailing ship; a huge model of the battleship *Missouri*; a replica of a wooden deck, complete with cannons and a modern flat-screen playing the battle scene from *Master and Commander*; ration cards from World War II; emotional paintings from various eras of Navy history.

As I wandered, I thought about letting go, about prying my determined fingers from my adult children's lives, about choosing a close relationship over having things turn out my way.

Always a curious child, Matt once took the entire set of encyclopedias into the bathroom when he took a bath and stacked them on the floor.

After he finally came out, he explained: "I like to do research, and if I just take the T encyclopedia into the tub to look up tigers, then I can't look up the other animals it talks about at the end of the article, like jaguars and cougars."

He and I were both happy when technology brought Wikipedia and links you could open with a simple click.

His curiosity led him to the engineering program at Oregon State University. By this time, he had transferred his passions to space and often said he hoped to be the first man on Mars.

Then one day he told us he would like to join the Air Force, viewing that as an eventual route into the space program.

He didn't really see the logic of the pacifist views he grew up with, he had decided, and this seemed like the smartest move for his future.

It was one of those "Mom moments" when you sense that maybe it would be best to wait before you say anything.

I was born into an Amish family and my husband into a Mennonite one, both Christian religious traditions that teach peace and "nonresistance"—a strict form of pacifism—and shun violence, revenge, lawsuits, and military service.

Both of Matt's grandfathers served in alternative service instead of the military—one at a veteran's hospital in Roseburg, Oregon, and the other in various capacities including working on a dairy farm and planting trees in Colorado.

The previous generations suffered much worse, since registering as a conscientious objector was not an option.

Mennonites are the first to grant the paradoxes in their position—and the moral dilemmas. Oddly, our culture shares many values with the military, such as respecting authority, doing your duty, and sacrificing for others. Also, we know there are plenty of Christians who feel as called to serve in the military as we do to avoid it.

Yet, we always come back to Jesus telling us to love our enemies, turn the other cheek, do good to them who hate us, and pursue a heavenly Kingdom that is not of this world.

When Matt told us what he was thinking, I had a choice. I could freak out, beg, manipulate with guilt, and haul out a list of bearded ancestors who sacrificed dearly for something he was tossing to the winds.

Or I could respect his decision and make our relationship more important than my disappointment.

I chose the latter.

Matt endured interviews, applications, and tests. He said, "I figured if I wasn't supposed to do this, God could close the door at any time." Now and then, he would call me. "Mom, I know how you feel about this, but would you mind praying for me today? I have an important interview coming up."

I would take a deep breath and pray for God's will to be done.

"Just so he won't be in a place with the Air Force where he's in danger," a friend said to me. I hadn't even thought about that. I was worried he'd be in a job where he'd put others in danger.

He assured me he probably would not.

Just when it looked like Matt would actually become an Air Force officer, he had to get a physical examination. He has a slight curve in his back. It was less than three degrees too big. He was disqualified.

We both wondered what God was up to.

Eventually, he was offered a civilian job with the Navy,

which meant he wouldn't exactly join the military, but, for a Mennonite mom, it's pretty much the same.

Since three of our six children are living in the East this year, Paul and I and the remaining three flew to Dulles International Airport on Christmas Day. We all had a few days together at a rented cabin.

One day, Matt drove us through unspeakable traffic and escorted us proudly around our nation's capital—to his house, the Navy Yard, and the Museum of American History. He bought us all coffee before we left the Navy Yard, and we sat at outdoor tables near a sign that said saluting is not mandatory in this area.

Over a turkey dinner at my sister's house, we talked about the path he's taken. Matt said, "Mom and Dad, I have to say you were exemplary in how you handled this."

I don't know if we were or not, but it was nice to hear.

Matt still gives his dad advice about electronics, and he chats with me on Skype. He knows we love him. We hug when we meet and leave. We find a lot to laugh about. He assures me his risk-taking teenage brother will be fine.

I pray for all my children but recognize that God does not need to check with me about how He operates in their lives. It is always tempting to try to control my adult children's decisions, but I do not regret choosing a close relationship over insisting Matt do things my way. And I think even the beard-ed ancestors, cooking over a fire at a Civilian Public Service camp, would tell me they see the sense in that.

The Final Pigtail

We should have had a party for "The Last Pigtail," called the rest of the family in, invited a few friends, and made a proper ceremony out of braiding Jenny's long, red hair for the last time and fastening it with the little balls-on-elastic pigtail holder.

But I didn't, because at the time I must have been too busy jerking her hair into a braid, making sure she had her lunch, and shooing her out the door.

And, of course, I had no idea it was the last one.

I found the pigtail holder lying on the bathroom counter a few days ago—two plastic, teal-colored balls on a brown elastic. Someone found it upstairs and tossed it into the bathroom, I'm guessing. I looked at it and thought, with sudden grief, *Wait. I don't do pigtails any more, do I? When did this happen? When did I stop?*

When you raise three Mennonite daughters with hair to their waists, you become skilled at doing hair, and you own brushes and barrettes and clips, elastics and pigtail holders by the basketful, combs and bands and bows, conditioners and detanglers and sprays.

We developed a whole vocabulary. School braids and Aunt Becky braids and Tia-buns and ponytails and French braids tucked up. We went through phases—from big lavish bows and lacy clips to minimal elastics to those little spring-loaded combs that bite with plastic teeth.

And, then, without warning, I was finished. My skills were no longer needed, and the bows and barrettes lay forgotten in

35

a drawer.

Jenny, the youngest of my six children, has her fourteenth birthday this month. Two months ago, she told me the time had come, and, now, with no help from me, she twirls her hair into a bun every morning and tops it with a chic, black, lace-trimmed prayer-veil in the Mennonite tradition, a sign that her faith in Jesus Christ is all her own.

Overnight, she is a quarter-inch taller than me, a lovely young lady in swishy skirts and heels. "One year and twenty days until I join the youth group," she says gleefully, "and two years and twenty days until I can drive."

I hold the little teal balls and stretch the elastic between my fingers and think about daughters growing up, about how little girls disappear and young women take their place, about how the world seems like an unwelcoming place and why is she so eager to face it, and how can I ever let her go?

Jenny as a little girl was always running, physically and mentally, her wild imagination barely keeping up with her tireless body. She would dash onto the porch, step on the rail, and leap out onto the trampoline four feet away, then jump off and climb up the fence and on to the top of the storage-shed roof to watch her teenage brothers play tackle football, while she pouted because I wouldn't let her join them.

She loved to learn new things, studied insects with fascination, read hundreds of books, and learned to embroider and to solve problems in her unique way. One day during this phase, our family took a day trip, and Jenny took her embroidery along. We were ready to head home in the van when Jenny said, "Isn't anyone going to sit in the front seat?"

"Apparently not," we said. "Why does it matter?"

"Because I lost my needle up there, and I was hoping someone would sit on it so I'd know where it was."

I've found that just when you think some lovable, little-girl trait is lost forever, it re-emerges in a different form.

Jenny had a ritual, every spring, of picking the first daffodils and taking a bouquet to each of the neighbors. "Has that little neighbor girl been by with flowers yet?" my neighbor Anita's daughter-in-law asked her the other week.

"No, she hasn't," Anita said. Telling me the story later, she added, "I think she may have outgrown that."

"I'm afraid so," I said.

But Jenny is still crazy about spring flowers. Only now, she lies on her stomach in the grass to photograph them, then turns the photos to artistic black-and-white with a vivid spot of color and posts them online.

The interest in embroidery expanded to needlework of all kinds. She sewed herself a daffodil-yellow skirt for Easter Sunday and wants to take a course in home economics.

She still climbs to the shed roof, not to watch her brothers, but to take pictures of herself, hands outstretched, appearing to grab a jet trail from the sky.

To me she seems vivid with possibility—in contrast to myself at that age, headed for bulimia and convinced that everyone would be happiest if I disappeared.

So, if I somehow survived, why do I have these dark fears for her?

The world these days can be a vicious place for young women, full of manipulation, lies, danger, and confusing messages.

Yes, she's tough and smart and quick-witted and fearless, but she's also female, young, vulnerable, and small.

And she has so terribly much to lose.

So we talk about boundaries and beauty and boys, about choices and trust and the Queen of England. Did the queen ever wear skimpy tops or t-shirts with suggestive messages? Why not? Because she has too much dignity and importance and self-respect. "Well, you have at least as much value and dignity as the queen. Remember that."

I believe that young women need men who respect and protect them, and I am grateful for Jenny's dad and brothers.

One morning, my husband unknowingly bumped his cell phone and called me on the way to school. Finally, I deciphered the distant voices on the other end. Jenny was asking Paul all about cars, and he was giving a long and technical explanation about how radiators work, as though there were no reason at all to think a thirteen-year-old girl wouldn't understand.

Jenny has no idea how blessed she is with such a dad—and with her big protective brothers.

I used to worry at times that Jenny was so cared for and everything was so easy for her that she would never learn empathy. But life has a way of teaching what we need to know, and she often prays for others and supports friends going through hard times.

At almost fourteen, Jenny sings in a children's choir, argues with her siblings, accessorizes endlessly, and dotes on her cats. She wants a real job this summer.

She will be different in subtle ways at sixteen, at eighteen, at twenty-one.

I probably will not recognize the last time she needs my help sewing a skirt, the last reminder to practice for choir, the last discussion about acne.

I will realize it later, finding a scrap of fabric behind the sewing machine or a forgotten folder of songs on the piano. That was the last time, back then, and I had no idea.

She is supposed to grow and change, to leave and become. I admit that. My calling is to stay and pray, as I stand in the bathroom and slowly stretch a little pigtail holder in my fingers, remembering the lively child who once was and celebrating the vivid woman who someday takes her place.

I've Got This

"**M**om? I have a little problem."

I walked into the kitchen to investigate. Fourteen-year-old Jenny was kneeling on the floor, holding a muffin tin. Twelve little piles of thick, blueberry-studded muffin batter lay in neat rows on the linoleum.

Jenny explained that there wasn't much room on the counter, so she had set the muffin tin "kind of on the edge," and when she plopped in the last of the batter, the entire tin flipped onto the floor. When she picked it up, the batter stayed. Now what?

This was another inevitable lesson in a summer of learning household skills: Handling Disaster. Specifically, what do you do about food on the floor?

I know someone who automatically tosses any food in any form that touches the floor and others who follow the five-second rule. I base my decision on a few specific questions, and now was as good a time as any for Jenny to learn to make this crucial judgment.

Is the floor clean? Yes, pretty much.

Are there expensive ingredients? Well, blueberries and more than a cup of sour cream, so yes.

Will it be heated? Yes, baked at 350 degrees, which ought to kill any germs.

Is it obviously ruined? No.

Will anyone know if we don't tell? No.

Alrighty then. What doesn't kill you makes you stronger. Scoop it up and put it in the oven.

She did. The muffins came out crumbly, sweet, warm, and

delicious, especially with the lemon glaze she dribbled on top.

No one knew of their perilous beginning until after they were all gone, less than a day later.

This is our summer of Practical Household Skills Training. Somehow, between lots of capable older siblings and a schedule full of academics and music, Jenny hadn't learned the tasks around the house that I thought a fourteen-year-old ought to know.

True, she gathered dirty laundry, emptied the dishwasher, and fed the cat, but was incapable of taking most domestic projects from start to finish.

"I still have *years*," she said, dismissing my anxious plans with the child's perspective that sees age eighteen as nearly as far off as gray hair.

"No, sorry, you don't," I said, knowing how quickly life changes in the upper-teen years.

So she is baking, mowing the lawn, sweeping and mopping floors, and sewing a zebra-print apron trimmed in a bright teal. We work on menus together. She tends her own garden.

She is having fun, at least some of the time. But, much more importantly, she is developing that confidence that comes from being able to take care of herself and her world.

The first time she made the muffins, she was tentative and fearful and almost in tears when they fell.

The second time, she acted calm and capable, and the muffins turned out well without the slightest trauma. The rest of us ate them and raved. Jenny looked pleased but not surprised. *Of course, they're amazing. I know what I'm doing.*

Often, it would be easier to do the chores myself than teach the children how. I remember sending Ben and Steven out to vacuum the van and then later sitting them down and taking the plugged-up vacuum cleaner apart in front of them.

"*This* is the hose. It is an inch and a half in diameter. It is designed to pick up dirt. It is not designed to pick up anything bigger than a marble, such as the popsicle sticks and navy-blue hair bows we are finding here, stuck in a wad of hair and dust."

Then there were the lectures on loading the dishwasher: "We note this serving spoon covered in sticky rice that someone put in the top rack. You must rinse off all the gloppy food before it goes in here or it will coat everything."

When I complained about this process—"Seriously, they ought to know this stuff by now!"—a friend told me I was a saint.

"Their future roommates will bless you," she insisted.

So I persisted.

I saw the importance of self-care skills in a new way when my mother broke her hip.

Always independent and hard-working like a good Amish woman should be, she was reduced to helplessness. A patient but determined therapist gave her the gift of dignity and capability, teaching Mom to once again walk to the bathroom, dress herself, brush her teeth, and put her hair up in a bun.

That same gift of dignity is what I want for my family: "I am not helpless. I can do this and do it well. I can figure it out."

Perhaps it's my Amish background that feeds my determination to teach my children. The Amish never got on the self-esteem trend in which children were told they were wonderful for simply being, rather than doing. I think the Amish always sensed that a healthy sense of self came from knowing you could handle this, you had what it took, and you had something to offer to others. And that came from adding skill to skill, from shelling peas as a small child to running a farm as an adult.

As a Mennonite, I don't go as far as my Amish ancestors. My six children don't know how to milk a cow, butcher a pig, or hitch a horse to a buggy.

But they can wash windows, address an envelope, iron a shirt, oil a squeaky hinge, set mousetraps, dress a wound, scrub a shower, follow a recipe, plan a route, replace a button, weed a garden, and wash a load of dark delicates.

It expands their future options, I hope. You can live much better in a poor economy, take a fulfilling volunteer position, or live in a remote area if you can cook beans in a crock pot, cut your own hair, and make your own clothes.

I haven't done a perfect or complete job. Steven still doesn't keep his room clean despite all the time I've invested in teaching him how. One daughter has never taken to cooking. I've been too divided by gender at times—the girls, I realize now, don't know enough about car maintenance or the boys about mending clothes. I obviously couldn't teach certain skills I never learned well myself.

But the successes are immensely gratifying. Eighteen-year-old Steven fills and stacks fifty-pound bags of grass seed all night, then comes home at 7:00 a.m. He cooks a batch of rice, chops a tomato and an onion, cracks five eggs into a skillet, pulls exotic spices from the cupboard, and artfully combines it all into an enormous, fragrant, nutritious breakfast.

"Do you need any help?" I say.

"Nope. I've got this. I'm good," he says, grinning. I sneak a bite when he's not looking. Delicious.

Jenny decides to transplant a few volunteer rutabagas into her little garden. Ben e-mails me for a cabbage salad recipe. Emily alters a secondhand dress to fit. We pick wild blackberries, and Jenny makes a cobbler.

"We can handle this," they say, without knowing they're saying it. "We can do this. We have something to offer."

Already, at times, I have the joy of hearing them say to others, "Here. Let me show you how. You can do it too. I'm sure you can. You have what it takes, I can tell."

Muffins, Limos, and Manageable Consequences

I've learned to be relieved when the cookies taste awful and the car runs out of gas.

It means my husband and I have managed, for the moment, to set the boundaries where our teenagers are making choices for themselves but the consequences are still manageable.

Parenting is terrifying mostly because the stakes are so high.

It's tempting for protective parents to make all the children's decisions. Or, similarly, to let kids choose but to protect them from any of the results.

At the other extreme, there's the chilling prospect of young people making increasingly unwise and unsupervised decisions until the doors to healthy future prospects close and lock, one by one.

So we search for a redemptive middle ground.

Jenny, our youngest child, celebrated her fifteenth birthday by having her cousin Allison over. The two of them decided to make a big batch of monster cookies for Jenny to take to school the next day, a birthday tradition at her private school.

Both girls are capable of baby-sitting, cleaning a bathroom, and cooking a meal, so I had no qualms about turning them loose to make cookies after I handed them the right jar of peanut butter.

I hadn't counted on the special insanity that happens when

two teenagers work on a project together.

"Oops! Hahahahaha!!"

"How much flour?"

"This recipe doesn't take flour!"

Waves of giggles.

The first batch into the oven oozed like a lava flow all over the cookie sheet.

They stirred in a cup of flour, but the next panful wasn't much better. "I'm sure it's that weird peanut butter," Jenny announced, hoping it was all my fault.

The mixing bowl went into the fridge to salvage later. We bought ice cream bars to take to school.

When I made the remaining cookies, the dough was sticky and heavy, like a science experiment demonstrating highly viscous liquid, a lot like . . . corn syrup.

That evening I asked Jenny, "How much corn syrup did you and Allison put into the cookie dough?"

She said, "I don't know. Whatever the recipe said. A cup and a half, I think."

The recipe called for one-and-a-half teaspoons.

"Oops," Jenny said.

Next time, she'll get it right.

Meanwhile, our nineteen-year-old son, Steven, was on a three-week road trip accompanied by two friends, meandering home from a friend's wedding on the East Coast by way of two cars and hospitable friends and relatives in Arkansas, Indiana, and other places. One of the cars was a 1996 Cadillac "funeral car," we were told, that an acquaintance bought on eBay and asked these guys to transport home from South Carolina.

We pictured a sleek, gray hearse with a swooping silver emblem on the side crossing Nebraska with Steven at the wheel, singing.

"No, no," Steven said, "not a hearse. Like, a limousine to take the family to the cemetery and back. With six doors." Either way, it was just the sort of quirky arrangement that Steven loves.

I prayed a lot about this trip, as texts from Steven were scarce and scary. "Where are you?" I sent one day, and soon got a reply: "Bottom of a canyon with a broken leg and I can't move."

Oh, Steven.

They came home, safe and grinning, on a Thursday evening. "Did anything unusual happen on your trip?" my husband asked Steven, who gives out information like my mom used to dole out spending money: seldom, sparsely, and like it causes great pain to part with it.

"No. Nah. Not really."

"Oh, yeah, we ran out of gas four times," Steven recollected, two days later. "I think there was something funny about the gas gauge in the limo. So after the first time we got this little gas can and kept some gas on hand."

Between monster-cookie rescues and prayers for safety, it's easy to forget that these are remarkably smooth waters. Many young people their ages face monstrous dilemmas where none of the options are pleasant and the consequences are almost unthinkable.

Sometimes it's through reckless decisions accumulating one by one, sometimes through others preying on their innocence, sometimes through lack of a guide—they all lead to situations no teenager should have to face.

The day Steven returned, my friend Ila and I took our church's Girls for God club to visit a pregnancy center and deliver the baby blankets and hats we had sewed at our club meeting the month before.

With fifteen girls aged nine to fourteen, we crowded into

the beautiful waiting room. Debbie, our tour guide and director of the clinic, told us about the wide range of services they provide.

"Our youngest client ever was ten years old," she said. Seventeen pairs of eyes stared at her, round with disbelief.

"Such innocence," commented Debbie wistfully, looking over our group.

"A third of our clients are under nineteen years old," she went on. "Almost every girl who walks in here for a pregnancy test has two things in common. She is scared to death, and she has no one to help her. No one. We try, first of all, to let her know that someone will be there for her."

I tried to picture Jenny and Allison, not giggling in the kitchen, but preyed on, possibly pregnant, alone, and terrified, facing adult decisions with the sketchy wisdom of ninth-graders.

No wonder we obsess about protecting them.

Two days after that, I noticed a news article about a young man who had been arrested. His name stirred a memory, and a bit of sleuthing confirmed it: He had sung in a children's choir with Steven, long ago when both of them were little and innocent. I used to chat with this boy's mom while we both waited on our kids to finish choir practice.

He faces at least five years in prison if convicted.

I have been to state prisons to help with cookie projects at Christmastime and a barbecued lunch for the inmates in the fall. Prison is a hard, harsh little universe of its own, sharp with tension, relentless in its daily realities. It always reduces me to tears and makes me come home and extract promises of lifelong, law-abiding behavior from my boys.

What steps would lead from little choirboy to possible inmate, I wondered. Was it one impulsive decision, a series of worsening choices, or a disturbed attempt to salve pain inflicted by others? No matter what or why, his steps had led to darker places and narrowing possibilities until suddenly they stopped in disaster and heartbreak.

As a parent, I want formulas. These rules, these words, these boundaries—and at the end of the fragile teenage years, capable people stepping into adulthood.

The scary truth is, much of it is out of our control. We are dependent on what we know at the moment, the grace of God, unseen compulsions in a child's soul, and the influence of many others.

So we try to let them experience results in doses they can handle. We let Steven figure out how to keep his car going, and we have Jenny make the recipe over again. We love deeply and pray a lot and believe in second chances. We apologize when we get it wrong. We sew burp rags for the pregnancy center and make Christmas cards for prisoners.

And we try to keep our eyes and hearts open for all the lost young people who need someone to say, "I am here for you; I believe in you; you're going to make it through."

Not Mine to Find or Fix

Maybe, I admitted afterwards while calming my knotted insides with a cup of tea, it wasn't my job to root, rubber-gloved, through the garbage. Maybe Ben's college degree and future career did not depend on that missing clear, plastic textbook wrapper with its elusive password, after all. Maybe it was up to him to find a way through this little crisis. Maybe it wasn't mine to fix.

But, unfortunately, I didn't realize that until later.

I used to think that by the time I had four children in their twenties, the house would be mostly quiet. I would have time to make quilts, and we could get by with a single pizza for dinner.

Instead, my independent and adventuresome offspring still go and come in such random patterns that, when people ask how many still live at home, I have to stop and count. Off they go to a few months of Bible school, to a year's volunteer work in other countries, to college. Then home again for a few months and off on the next quest.

At the moment, five of my six live at home. The best thing about this is their lively company, especially the entertaining repartee, such as:

"You should sing on the radio," Ben says after hearing Steven sing cheerfully.

"Why?" Steven says.

"So we could change stations," Ben says.

Or this:

"People with British accents are taken much more seriously than people with Southern accents," Emily says.

"Yes," Jenny says. "Unless they're people with Southern accents and a gun."

And:

"Somebody, put the ketchup in something attractive," I say while preparing Sunday dinner.

"Here, Steven, open wide," Emily says.

I laugh at them and think indulgent motherly thoughts about what astonishingly bright children we've been blessed with, so gifted and quick.

And then, in the next minute, they make me frightened and frantic, because they are all making adult decisions, and they insist on being independent and self-assured in this as well. As opposed to the obvious and wise alternative: asking me what they should do, taking careful notes with a yellow pencil, and saying, "Yes, Mom, absolutely," as they humbly follow each bulleted point.

I think the boys ought to cut their hair and the girls should eat more nutritious snacks. I want this one to get a better job and that one to send in his Bible school application. I take note of nice, well-behaved, potential future in-laws and make weighted suggestions.

Even though, in reality, none of it is mine to manipulate.

Twenty-year-old Ben spent a year volunteering in the big city of Toronto, and came home in September, just in time to begin another year at Linn-Benton Community College.

As a future engineer, his textbooks are enormous and expensive. *Physics for Scientists & Engineers: A Strategic Approach* (Third Edition) came in the mail one day, and Ben tore the five-pound book out of its package. The next day, he discovered that the wrapper was supposed to contain a little paper with a password to a corresponding website, crucial to the course.

He had, of course, ripped off the plastic wrapper and tossed it away. Buying another password would cost more than sixty dollars.

What I wonder now is, *Why did I snatch at this problem as mine to fix and completely obsess about it?* Maybe because he is a poor student, fresh off the mission field.

Ben and I pawed through the clean and paper-filled office garbage and the slightly slimy kitchen wastebaskets with no success. I reached around him without asking and scrolled down the Amazon page on his laptop, looking for information, and then insisted that he call his instructor and ask for advice.

Ben calmly said he didn't think that was necessary and listed his reasons. I thought he was foolish and stubborn, and I hoped savagely that his sweet girlfriend would see this infuriating side of him before he ever proposed to her.

Then, desperate, we donned protective gloves and dug through the days-old trash in the barrel outside, picking through old meat wrappers and soggy tissues and far worse.

We didn't find it.

My husband tried to slip an occasional word of advice to me as I pursued this frantic quest: "Let it go. Let him worry about it. It isn't your problem."

Of course, he was right, which I didn't admit until the search was over and I saw that I was obsessed beyond all rational reason.

How embarrassing.

I have been teaching a Sunday school class in which we study women of the Bible. The parallels to us today are astonishing, especially that recurring resolve: "Nothing is happening here, so I need to take action. This is entirely mine to fix."

The childless Abraham and Sarah in the Book of Genesis were solemnly promised a son but were still infertile, so, after years of waiting, Sarah got the bright and improbable notion that Abraham could have a child with the servant girl and all would be well. The servant did have a son, but all was very much not well, and the generations to follow paid dearly for Sarah's manipulation.

Their daughter-in-law, Rebekah, was determined that her second-born son, Jacob, would receive the ceremonial blessing. She used trickery, scheming, and outright lies to make it happen. She paid for it by sending Jacob away for his own safety and never seeing him again.

"Dear me, can't you see this would have worked out if you had just trusted God and waited a bit longer?" I say to these long-ago women as I study the lesson at the kitchen table on Sunday mornings.

But Scripture has a way of speaking right back at me. What about trying to rescue Ben from his own carelessness? Or the probing questions I ask the kids who don't talk enough? Or all the hints, tinged with accusation, that I toss their way, knowing it's theirs to figure out but also utterly certain that things won't work out unless I step in.

"Be quiet. Trust me. Wait. Just enjoy them—your gifts from Me." That's what I hear from God when they're all asleep and I sit with a pot of tea and my Bible in the early quiet.

All right then. If You say so. After all, Ben figured out a way to get that crucial password without any help from me.

On the way to church, Steven, who is not into arson or smoking, has a match dangling from his mouth. Emily asks, logically, "Why do you have a match in your mouth?"

Steven mumbles, "I'm gonna set the church on fire. On fire for God."

After church, the match is still there. I think, "Oh please!" and other admonishing motherly things I want to say, but I don't say them.

Emily says, "You setting the church on fire?"

"Nope," Steven says. "Just looking striking."

I laugh, which is, in the end, the best response to these remarkable young adults of mine—far better than anxious manipulating, endless hinting, or digging through garbage for something that was never mine to find.

2.

Change:

Sandals to Snow Boots, Heels to Orthopedics

The Books Must Stay

Every day, I get e-mails from a woman who calls herself FlyLady. She tells domestically challenged and ADD people like me exactly what to do each day so we're in control of our houses instead of the other way around. She tries to keep us from getting distracted with alphabetizing the recipes when we should be emptying the dishwasher.

"Shine your sink," FlyLady says. "Put on your lace-up shoes."

Not your normal get-organized to-do list, but, if you step out in faith and do what she says, you find that it works.

FlyLady constantly tells us to get rid of things we don't use or love.

"Toss, toss, toss," she says, and reminds us to dash around the house on a "Fling-Boogie," picking up twenty-seven items to toss or give away. Clutter is our enemy, she insists.

So with shoes firmly on my feet, I picked through my sewing patterns and put dozens of vintage-1980s dress and skirt patterns in the Goodwill box. I sorted through my twelve-year-old daughter's closet and weeded out two bags of outgrown clothes.

"Oooh, this was so cute on you!" I said, but I resolutely folded it into the bag and passed it on to a friend with two young girls.

I even gritted my teeth and tossed the children's liquid Tylenol from 2008. I knew that the predicted major earthquake might hit Oregon tomorrow, and my son might be moaning with a broken leg, trapped under a limb from the walnut tree, cut off from all medical care and unable to swallow Tylenol tablets.

But I tossed it anyhow.

Old candles to St. Vincent de Paul. Torn pillowcases. I even got rid of a few Christmas card photos from two years ago.

Then it was time to organize the books.

We are a family who reads. We have bookshelves in bedrooms and a wall of books in the office and books stacked under beds and on top of nightstands. There are books on the coffee table and in backseats of cars and up in the attic.

Even I could tell they were getting out of hand, multiplying like rabbits in dark corners, filling desktops and headboards and closets.

All right, FlyLady, I would toss, viciously and lavishly.

I started on my half of the wall of shelves in the office. "Not the books by people I know," I said, sliding them safely to the left.

"But are they any good?" my daughter Emily asked.

"Some are, some aren't, but I'm keeping them." I couldn't toss the books any more than I could toss the friendships that went with them.

Nor could I donate the Zits comic books the kids give me for Mothers Day. Or the Oregon hiking guides. Or all the good stories I reread at least once a year.

The guilt books, the earnest kind that you ought to read because they claim to be helpful and beneficial, but you never get it done—those needed to go. *Creative Home Decorating, German Through Pictures, the Western Garden Book, Saving Your Pastor from Spiritual Disaster, Survival for Busy Women.*

Decorating ideas can be found online, I decided. I have no prospects of visiting Germany or an Amish Sunday morning service. My garden is what it is, books or no books.

If my pastor husband is headed for disaster, I probably

can't save him anyhow. And I'm too busy to read Survival for Busy Women.

Toss, toss, toss.

My bookshelves looked like they could breathe again. Really, that wasn't so bad.

It was time to face the children's books.

A large bookcase in the upstairs hall hosted them, all alphabetized from Louisa May Alcott's *Little Men* to Gertrude Chandler Warner's line of The Boxcar Children.

The shelves were packed, with extra books shoved sideways on top of others and piled beside the bookcase.

FlyLady perched on my shoulder, heartlessly whispering, "Toss, toss, toss."

Amelia Bedelia? No, no, that good woman and her earnest literalness had to stay. As did all the "Mandie" books that Amy devoured at age eleven, competing frantically with her cousin Jessi.

The Ramona books that Paul read to the children at bedtime—definitely keeping those. And *The Great Brain*. And *Anne of Green Gables*.

"Toss anything you don't use or love," FlyLady always says. Well, I loved them all, but I had to do something.

I checked. Yes, there was room on that wall for two bookcases instead of one. Feeling more clever than FlyLady, for once, I went hunting on Craigslist.

Finally, after hours and days of dead ends and unanswered e-mails, fate smiled. A family in Albany still had a set of two tall, matching oak-trimmed bookcases.

While my husband fetched them in the van, the girls and I emptied out the old bookcase, carried it away, and cleaned up the years of dust behind it.

We set up the new bookshelves, side by side, open and welcoming, ready for all our old friends.

The first shelf from the bottom I set high enough that all the old picture books could stand in a row. Richard Scarry, kids' atlases, *Mother Goose.*

Soon we were sitting on the floor, my daughters and I, happily distracted, paging through the old books and remembering.

I wonder, what is it about books? The little lacy dresses in bins in the attic have a sentiment of their own, as do the Duplos®, the Teddy bears, the old highchair.

But books bring it all back in a different way. I pick up a tattered, blue book and am back on that old, brown-plaid couch up in Canada in July, the Indian paintbrush blooming orange in the meadow outside the front door, nursing the new baby, with a red-headed two-year-old snuggled close, singing our way through "Old MacDonald Had a Farm" with a baa baa here and a moo moo there.

Here were Sam the cat and Dudley the bumbling pig from *Richard Scarry's Great Big Mystery Book,* trying to catch thieves such as the sinister Blackfinger Wolf, who perched on the handle of a shopping cart and rode it "down into the lower part of town, down where all the robbers lived."

Ben's favorites: *Bears on Wheels,* where he first evidenced his love for numbers (five bears on five wheels, then one on one again), and *Barney Beagle Plays Baseball,* perhaps the seed for his love of sports of all kinds.

The one Matt had memorized word-perfect at three years old, where Chris and Matt, the mouse brothers, bring home a tadpole, which grows into a bullfrog that takes over their dad's armchair and eats all the food in the house. I still find myself quoting, "'I am a growing frog,' said Bullfrog," when the teenage boys eat up all the leftovers in the fridge and the cake I was saving for the potluck.

"Oh, this one! I remember this!" we said, stroking the old

pages. The crazy Dr. Seuss books we still know by heart. "Yertle the turtle was king of the pond," and "I want a long tail just like Lolla-Lee-Lou."

Going to Sleep on the Farm, Jenny's favorite, which I read to her at bedtime, hoping to put her to sleep as all the animals dropped off one by one, but instead it was always me yawning and struggling to keep my eyes open.

And the unforgettable "Frances" books, where Frances the badger overcomes her obsession with bread and jam and gains a bit of victory over Thelma the ultimate frenemy—long before the word was coined—sometimes with a little help from a wise mom but usually on her own, which is how it ought to work. "No backsies on this." Who could ever forget that line?

It was a long time before we finally left the memories of snuggled reads on old couches in long-ago houses and arranged the books in a neat row along the bottom of the new bookcases.

Up above, we arranged the precious chapter books, all in order.

"A time to keep, and a time to throw away," the Book of Ecclesiastes says.

The extra can opener can go, as well as the ought-to books, the skirt from five pounds ago, the ceiling-light covers we may or may not need again.

But the children's books and the memories are mine to keep and here to stay.

New Trees and Option C

O ur home has a new look this spring, encircled by a dozen saplings, leafy and very much alive.

I suppose it began when the oak tree fell. Old and massive, it had stood there for some two hundred years, and then on a November evening it broke off at the base and gently lay down, draping one heavy arm over our unfortunate van and spreading gnarly fingers up the sidewalk almost to the house.

The pine trees, much younger than the oak but already almost as tall, were planted by my husband's parents some thirty years ago. They bought them, I am told, because they were very inexpensive—from a nursery salesman who conveniently forgot to mention that each tree would shed roughly a million long, poky needles every fall.

Our children hated those pine trees. The eight-inch-long needles stabbed bare feet, clogged the gutters along the roof, and piled up in the flowerbeds. You couldn't pick them up with the lawn mower, so we raked them up about five times every fall.

Paul and the children soon were clamoring for great changes in the Smucker landscape. We survived losing the oak tree, so why not get rid of all the pine trees, they said, and plant new ones?

Mom?

I said no.

It took years for this house, uprooted and moved to this lot in 1979, to lose that naked look. Now the oak tree was gone, exposing the east side of the property, and, nasty needles or

59

no, I didn't want the rest of the big trees gone.

"We can research different kinds of trees and find something we would all like," Paul said.

"Give me a few years, OK?" I said.

Paul and the children regrouped and changed their tactics. Loud arguments, they have found, work with everyone but me. They became subtle and gentle, like herding sheep into a stock trailer, slowly circling the perimeter of the field with a broom in hand so the sheep hardly know they're there. Gradually, the sheep move toward the trailer, thinking it's their own, original idea.

"OK," I said. "The spindly tree by the lilacs can go. And that crippled maple that the lawn mower ran into. And one pine tree. Just one."

While we were gone camping at the coast, our appropriately nicknamed friend, Chip, cut down the southwest tree and tidied up afterward.

"See, Mom? That's not so bad!"

"It leaves a big, obvious hole," I said.

The gentle pressure resumed. Paul and the children wanted all the pine trees gone. I did not. My family was kind and sweet and subtle, but I felt like we were at a revival meeting, and I was the last one to go forward to give my heart to Jesus, and they were all trying to encourage me without coming on so strong that I bolted and ran out the door.

Somehow, I saw it all in terms of winning and losing. Their way or mine. Weak or strong. Conqueror and vanquished.

"OK," I finally snapped. "You win and I lose. Cut them down."

"It's not about winning and losing," Paul said, "unless you decide to make it that way."

"Yes it is," I said, then added, still bitter after thirty years, "It's like the broccoli conversation. You always have to win."

I was referencing the time, now an often-retold part of our family history, when Paul ate lunch at my house while we were dating, and I cut fresh broccoli into florets and served them with a dip. He ate the bushy parts but left the stems. I said, "Why don't you eat the stems?" And he shot back, "Why should I? Do you eat tree trunks?"

This twisted logic befuddled me completely.

"No," I said slowly, certain that his comparison didn't work somehow, but I couldn't figure out what was wrong with it. It took me two days to figure out that we don't eat tree leaves, either, and even longer to forgive him.

Paul didn't say it was unfair to insert the broccoli episode into the current debate. He just said, a bit embarrassed, "I wasn't trying to win, you know. I was trying to be clever and funny to impress you. And the truth is, I never ate fresh broccoli and I didn't know you were supposed to eat the stems."

Oh. OK.

We agreed to do some research, together, or what kind of trees we would both like.

Meanwhile, unbeknownst to us, a nursery not far away had a batch of potted trees that hadn't sold, and they kept blowing over. So they told their employees that the trees were theirs for the taking and what didn't go would get destroyed.

One of the employees was Susan, who owned a pig. She happened to sell this pig to Paul's cousin Darrell and told him about the free trees. Darrell got some for himself.

Paul called Darrell about borrowing his chainsaw. Darrell thought, *Hmmm. Chainsaw. To cut down trees. That he might need to replace.*

Darrell told Paul about the free trees.

Paul called me. I said, "Sure. What can we lose?"

So Paul and Darrell fetched four trees for us, two maples already about twenty feet tall and two pines that shed their needles, but needles that are tiny and soft.

They were beautiful trees, the maples in particular.

At my urging, Paul went back with the van and trailer and got ten more.

We took out the old trees and put in the new. Paul ran hoses and faithfully watered, all summer, tree to tree.

They all survived, and this spring they obligingly leafed and needled out like they were here to stay, to grow, to make this place more beautiful than ever.

We are all happy with these trees, so why, I wonder, do I so readily think in fixed terms of win or lose, your way or mine, good and bad?

The Gospels tell us how the Pharisees confronted Jesus with a question: "Is it right for us to pay taxes to Caesar or not?" "A or B, which is it?" they seemed to be saying, ready to trap Him either way.

Jesus responded with Option C, a clear truth that transcended the petty competition.

"Give back to Caesar what is Caesar's and to God what is God's," He said, and then there was nothing more to say.

There's usually an Option C in any debate when we forget about winning and losing, your way vs. mine.

We all give a little, we all listen, and we suddenly find twenty-foot trees, free for the taking, that will generously shade us all equally in summers to come.

How Fun to Turn Fifty

Now that I'm fifty years old, it takes me longer to catch on to things. Not that I've ever been quick on the uptake, as my exasperated siblings reminded me often when I was a child, but the machinery has slowed even more the past few years.

A month or so before my birthday, a man in a UPS uniform addressed me as "young lady." I was flattered. I heard it a second time just a few days later from a helpful employee in a home-improvement store.

Young lady, indeed, I thought. *If he only knew.*

It took about a day and a half for the obvious truth to dawn.

A: This was a new development, to be thus addressed; or, at least, it hadn't happened for many years.

B: My hair is going gray.

C: AARP sends me letters.

D: Therefore—hellooo, as my teenagers say—I could probably assume . . . "young lady" is a euphemism for "old lady."

I had a good laugh at myself.

This is one of the best things about turning fifty—I can keep myself endlessly entertained with my own blunders and quirks. Thirty years ago, I would have been horrified. Now, it's hilarious.

If this keeps up, I'll never lack for things to laugh at the rest of my life.

We did not have a big party on my birthday since I still felt half-dead from jet lag, having just returned from three weeks in Thailand. My husband took me out to dinner—or tried to—at Olive Garden, where I ate two bites of my exquisitely cheesy ravioli in Alfredo sauce and thought I was going to throw up. We boxed it up to enjoy later and left hurriedly. I slept all the way home.

A month later, I celebrated at my friend Anita's house with a cozy tea party with her and my sister-in-law, Lois, whose fiftieth birthday was four days before mine.

We topped each other's stories of things forgotten and repeated, and chuckled as much at each other as at ourselves.

"Half-zheimers, I call it," Lois said. "Not quite Alzheimer's, but getting there."

At fifty, the president is close to your age, doctors look the age of your children, and servers in restaurants are mere infants. You remember history from when it happened—the Cold War, the Berlin Wall coming down, the day Reagan was shot, Challenger exploding. People expect a bit less of you and forgive a bit more.

And, inevitably, you are wiser than you were.

The small stuff doesn't matter so much now—the size of your nose, the people who don't like you, and getting sick when your husband takes you out to dinner.

But the big stuff—that matters a lot.

We discussed this, Lois and Anita and I—how the lives we have today are an accumulation of the choices we've made. Our relationships, health, finances, happiness, and spiritual maturity—or lack of them—all represent hundreds of decisions we made that grew into the shape and size of our current lives.

Naturally, then, much of our conversation centered around our adult children. It terrifies us to see them blithely make choices whose inevitable consequences are visible to us but not to them.

We talk to each other about this, but not so much to our

children. By age fifty, you learn the futility of endless lecturing. Some things children have to learn for themselves, so we confide in other moms, who make clucking, sympathetic noises. We know these lessons are theirs to learn, but it's not easy. Let me get you more tea.

And, yet, we admit as well, plenty of times we've been wrong.

Over the years we've seen everyone around us in a lather, devoutly pro or con, about a certain crisis, person, or product; candidate, book, or threat; fashion, scientific discovery, or religious revelation. We discussed and panicked or promoted as thoroughly as everyone else.

Somehow, the world kept turning and the crisis faded, the facts proved otherwise, and the book showed up at garage sales. And we all looked silly. But we can laugh about it now, most of the time.

This is another wonderful thing about age fifty: seeing the end of the story.

You can stay up late and get through the sad chapters of a novel before morning, but life stories take a long time to unfold, and people can be stuck in grief or injustice or mystery for years.

At fifty, I've lived long enough to see healing come to loved ones and justice to the silent sufferers. I've seen private sins come to light at last and hidden sacrifice rewarded. I've seen redemption for the ugliest situations and impossible dilemmas resolved.

It's a good thing to live long enough to say, with confidence, "It will all work out, trust me," and "I know it's hard, but you just avoided many bitter nights of regret."

We were at our prime in high school, or so we thought. As we classmates reach each new decade we send each other commiserating notes. "Not gonna talk about that number," we say, "but hope you have a good birthday."

Recently I found an old photo of myself at sixteen, a forlorn little face hidden behind enormous glasses.

What were we thinking, that that was the peak of our lives? In truth, we didn't know much, and there was no way to move but up.

I figure I'm starting the second half of my life, thanks to the marathon genes of my grandma, who still wrote letters at 103, and my dad, who cuts wood and writes his memoirs at ninety-five.

Strangers may patronize me and my children may laugh indulgently, but I plan to enjoy the next fifty years. There are places to explore, books to read, quilts to sew, friends to make—and plenty of work to do and things to laugh about.

I want to fear less, to say "no" without explaining, and to live long enough to discover the endings of a thousand more stories.

I see the coming years like Olive Garden's Alfredo sauce or tea at a friend's table. I've never yet had too much. I'm eager for many more.

The Story Goes On

This is what really happened, we were told during the open-mike time at the wedding reception, by a friend who may or may not have been exaggerating.

Janet, my niece, lived with her roommate, Judith, in the teachers' cottage near the Mennonite school just outside Sioux Lookout, Ontario. One evening, Mark was next door, enjoying a barbecue with a bunch of friends.

After a while, the guys noticed smoke was pouring out of the kitchen windows of the teachers' house. They looked at each other.

"You think we should do something?"

"Yeah, I guess."

Shrug.

Just then, they saw the door burst open as Janet ran out, flapping her hands and screaming, "Help! Somebody help me!"

Mark took off running. Without a word, he barged into the smoky kitchen, grabbed a dish towel, threw it over the grease fire on the stove, and smothered it.

Then he calmly went back to the barbecue.

A few of us, listening, thought, *He threw a dish towel on a grease fire?* But obviously it had worked, in more ways than one.

"Mark is a man of action," the friend said. "And few words."

Despite Mark's reticence, he managed to combine brave actions with enough convincing words, and eventually we got a pretty invitation to a wedding in Ontario. And there we were, eating homemade cake and sipping coffee at tables decorated in simple touches of blue and listening to the friend's version of what happened back toward the beginning.

Mark grew up in Ontario, and that's where they planned to live, Janet said, so that's where they decided to have the wedding, instead of her hometown in Minnesota. Plus it would solve most of the potential immigration hassles.

They are both people of practicality and getting things done without a lot of fuss.

We traveled to Canada—friends and family from Minnesota, my brother Fred from Oklahoma, my sister Rebecca from Virginia, our family from Oregon, other relatives from scattered points in the United States and Canada.

We gathered in Sioux Lookout, a small town in the northwestern part of Ontario, where landing float planes ripple the clear blue of the lake and beavers slap their tails and everything to the north is vast kilometers of wilderness—or bush, as they say in Canada.

This was more than a niece's wedding, more than a nostalgic trip for Paul and me to the area where we lived when the kids were small, more than a family gathering.

It was redemption and restoration and healing.

It's hard to describe how my nephew Leonard's suicide, six years ago, affected his family—his parents, his two sisters, and the extended family.

Shattered, maybe. Decimated. Broken.

True, we were all Christians. We believed in redemption. But this, it seemed, was beyond all recovery. It felt like the end of the story, far too soon, all emptiness and loss and doors shutting and dangling threads.

Pain followed pain. Janet, Leonard's younger sister, had a ruptured appendix. Annette, his older sister, and her husband, Jay, struggled with infertility. Promising adoption possibilities suddenly failed, bringing a new and aching grief.

Leonard's parents and sisters clung to one another for strength in the grief that seemed it would never abate. In the larger family, we slowly regained our footing and looked on, offering prayers but knowing there was nothing we could do to make it all better again.

The years passed. Each member of Leonard's family chose, deliberately, to keep going, to invest in others, to work hard, to be passionate about things that mattered, to laugh.

Then one day, there was Mark, who had Leonard's love for the outdoors and could have matched him at a hard day's work, and who loved Janet and would cheerfully have given his life to protect her.

Janet posted pictures online, all of them radiating joy.

Sensing a breeze of hope and blossoming restoration, we planned our route to the wedding.

Then, in June, we got the wildly ecstatic news that Annette and Jay were on their way to Florida to pick up a baby boy who was available for adoption.

We aunts and cousins who had prayed and longed on their behalf now wept for joy, mobbed the photos on Facebook, sent e-mails all in capital letters, and generally went crazy.

So we gathered in Sioux Lookout, where the sun shone on stiff pines and shivering birch and a deep, blue lake, while the wedding party posed for pictures on the dock. Mark stood on the very edge in his tux to tease Janet, who satisfyingly snapped at him, "Get away from there!"

Little Justice, the new nephew and youngest of the wedding party, so named because of what his parents want him to pursue in life, came down the aisle propped up in a red wagon.

My brother walked his beautiful daughter down the aisle, and they exchanged a long hug before he let her go. We aunts in the second row burst into tears right on cue and pawed in our purses for tissues.

We celebrated at a frou-frou-free reception, where the candles were circled in ribbons but not bows as per Janet's taste, and friends told stories of Mark taking decisive action and of Janet talking dramatically. We laughed, Janet and Mark grinned at each other romantically, and we all said, "Awww" and cried a little.

Then Annette took the mike and told of what the family had been through and of the sense of healing and restoration on this very special day.

She quoted a verse from the Book of Joel, where God promises, "I will repay you for the years the locusts have eaten."

That evening my sister and I finally got to spend time with little Justice. We held him close and touched his black, ringletted hair with our fingertips. Rebecca said she felt deeply invested in this child because of all the nights she lay awake praying for that one special child for Jay and Annette—"Please, God. *Please.*"

Mark and Janet left for a simple honeymoon in a northern cabin, and the rest of us made our way back to our scattered homes.

Of course, weddings are always beautiful, and so are babies, and families together, sitting around a living room with half the people on the floor, comfortable, talking and laughing and taking endless pictures.

But when you have been through shattering loss and years of recovery, it's not just a wedding, a baby, a family gathering.

It's one breathtaking gift after another, divine symbols that the story actually does, unbelievably, miraculously, at last, go on.

Changing My Ways But Not Missing Out

I ran into a relative on a recent Saturday night. He was my late cousin Sylvia's grandson, Floyd, a congenial Mennonite pastor from Iowa, who flew to Oregon to officiate at a wedding we attended. I found him at the reception and caught up on family news from the Midwest.

I am one of forty-eight grandchildren on the Yoder side. Floyd is one of probably five hundred great-great-grandchildren.

While we chatted, a young server came by and set a piece of cake in front of him. Floyd was happy to see he'd gotten a corner piece with lots of swirly, white icing. "Most people don't like the corner pieces," he said. "But I love all that frosting."

He paused.

"I get that love of sweets from the Yoders, you know. I remember visiting Barbara—your grandma, my great-great—and someone served her a banana. She peeled it, and then she sprinkled sugar on it before she ate it."

We laughed. Barbara was unforgettable.

"And how old was she when she died?" Floyd said. "A hundred and . . . ?"

"Four," I said. "Or actually two months shy of it."

We talked some more, and then I went home, leaving Floyd to enjoy his cake in peace, and treated myself to a high-protein, low-carb snack of celery sticks and natural peanut butter.

My grandma almost reached 104 years old, and my parents are well into their nineties, on a typical Midwestern-Amish diet.

I was taught to sprinkle brown sugar on my oatmeal for breakfast and white sugar on the sliced tomatoes we ate daily in late summer, along with sliced cucumbers mixed with cream and onions and, yes, a dash of sugar. Most meals were followed by cake or pie or pudding. As a teenager, I baked thousands of oatmeal or chocolate chip cookies for the family.

My mom still loves cinnamon rolls for breakfast and a dessert after supper.

I have carried on many of the family traditions—although I prefer salt on tomatoes—and added a few of my own.

I enjoy baking and always thought that the cookie dough in the mixing bowl was much better than the finished cookies, so I would indulge in just one more spoonful as I filled another cookie sheet.

Any combination of peanut butter and chocolate is my idea of heaven on earth. I make a fresh blueberry pie that, I am proud to say, my brother-in-law Chad from Pennsylvania claimed would be worth driving to Oregon for. I've made three-layer pumpkin cakes for Thanksgiving dinners, and innumerable chocolate crazy cakes for church potlucks, and layered cream-cheese-and-pudding desserts for guests.

My husband's family wasn't much different from mine. His great-grandma Annie, who from pictures and stories seemed to be a plump, cheerful, hearty woman, was known as "Corn Candy Grandma" because she always carried corn candy in the hidden pockets of her full, plain dresses and handed it out to the youngsters.

Last week my husband and I attended a fundraiser dinner at the Mennonite Home in Albany. Since the ambitious patriarch of the clan, Frank Kropf, instigated the nursing home's beginning, they invited his descendants to contribute to building a new development in the next few years.

Each of our place mats was printed with a brief history and a picture of Frank and Annie, and we were served a delicious dinner from the *Kropf Cookbook*. In the center of the table, in honor of Annie, corn candy was liberally sprinkled around a basket of mums.

I took some of the corn candy home for the children. It lay on the kitchen counter for two days.

I didn't eat the candy because I am trying to improve my eating habits, a difficult undertaking for anyone, but, for someone of Amish or Mennonite extraction, I'm convinced that it's three times as hard.

In fact, we like to keep pretty much everything the same as it's always been. As the old joke says: How many Mennonites does it take to change a light bulb?

Answer: "Change?"

An alternate answer is: "Eight. One to change the bulb and seven to make the meal."

This is the trouble with changing. It goes against habit, tradition, custom, and what worked for everyone else. It is said that we do the work of changing our ways only when the pain of change is less than the pain of staying the same.

I had always thought I would live to be as old as Grandma Barbara, having inherited much of her constitution, including her low blood pressure.

Besides, there was so much to get done in life it would take me at least a hundred years to do half of it.

But, at half her age, I was already feeling old and tired. Too often, I sounded like the letters my aunts used to write, about aches and vitamins and going to the chiropractor.

True, I had enough responsibilities to exhaust anyone, but getting through the day shouldn't feel like wading knee-deep in peanut butter.

I don't mind consequences when they happen to other people. In fact, it's possible that I have looked heavenward and thanked God when one of my teenagers finally got the traffic ticket he richly deserved.

The consequences in my own life were harder to face, but finally I admitted that the traditional Amish-Mennonite diet wasn't working for me. "Just omit white flour and sugar," a dieting friend said, as though it were that easy.

My sister-in-law Laura, deep into a slow, sensible weight-loss program, had a different approach.

It was important not only to cut out the "whites," she said, but also to wait a few hours between meals and eat fats and carbohydrates separately.

Most importantly, it was about replacing the bad stuff with something better—lots of good proteins and plenty of vegetables—and not going hungry.

That was the key information I had needed all those times I indulged in sugary goodies and knew I shouldn't. I had only seen what I shouldn't do. I hadn't looked at something positive I could eat instead.

So I followed her advice. Almost a month in, I do not see dramatic changes, only a gradual sense of things improving.

Someday, I hope to develop the temperance that will let me indulge in a single corn candy without grabbing a handful. For now, I abstain entirely.

Meanwhile, I find this true of necessary changes: I go into it thinking it will mean missing out on everything, sitting alone in the cold while everyone else celebrates.

The reality is quite different. I can still attend the wedding, admire the decorations, visit with the cousin, hug the bride, and laugh at the groomsmen's speeches.

The only real difference is eating a bit more fruit instead of that piece of cake. I discover that I am encouraged by my strength of will and also genuinely happy for my cousin, who is still young and healthy enough to enjoy the corner piece with its generous swirls of frosting.

On Love, Weddings, and Stormy Weather

O n a nasty winter evening we pulled our wedding dress-es out of sewing-room closets and from under beds, slid them into clean garbage bags, and brought them to Ros-ie's house, along with teapots, fruit trays, and the fixings for a chocolate fountain.

Rosie hooked the hangers onto the heavy curtain rods above the picture windows on the west side. The dresses hung in a long row of hope—pure white, cream, yellowed with age. Tucks, buttons, gathers. Plain capes, ruffles, a row of covered buttons. Long skirts, just-below-the-knee skirts, satins and cottons and tone-on-tone flowers. A sleek cascade of cream-colored lace.

To the left hung Great-Aunt Alice's, a simple knit dress, with cutwork on the bodice, that she wore at her wedding on the beach in Hawaii—love and marriage having arrived later in life when a big church wedding wasn't a high priority.

Rachel's was the fanciest of all, a heavy mass of late-eight-ies beads and gathers and ruffles, with a big bow on the back.

"The only one I would wear, right now, is Annie's," said our daughter Emily, scanning them all and indicating the inno-cent eyelet dress from the seventies with a rounded yoke and long, gathered skirt.

The three brides-to-be sat at one end of the living room just below three of the dresses. They smiled in a glowing haze of joyful expectation while the rest of us handed our gifts to Rosie's bright little girls, who wore the pink-and-cream dresses that their cousins, one of them now a bride, had worn to their mother's wedding. We hugged aunts and in-laws, bustled to the kitchen with our food, and found seats in the crowded living room.

"Have you ever seen the likes of all these weddings?" we asked each other. "No!" "Never!" Three weddings in the Smucker family in three months' time. Seven weddings altogether of young people we know well, involving, with some overlap—two nieces, one nephew, six of my husband's former students, numerous friends of our children, lots of former little Sunday School students and Bible Memory Campers—ranging in age from twenty to twenty-four and suddenly engaged to be married.

I feel like my Aunt Vina must have when my sister and I were at this stage: "These little girls," she had said in disbelief, "they actually think they're getting married!"

"This is not going to be a normal bridal shower," announced my sister-in-law Rosie, Paul's youngest sister. "We're all Smuckers, so, first of all, we're going to sing." And we did. Hymns, in fact, sung with the astonishing volume and skill for which Smuckers are known.

Outside, the drenching rain fell and the cold statistics blew—60 percent of marriages at this age end in divorce, according to the National Center for Health statistics.

Inside, we radiated hope and happiness.

It was time to share the advice we had brought for the brides.

"Forgiveness is really important," said Jolene, herself not so far removed from being a newlywed. "Just letting go of the past and not hanging onto it."

Annie said, "Some of the best advice I ever got was this: Focus on what is, rather than on what is not."

The brides smiled politely. Their mothers nodded solemnly. Yes. Mmm-hmmm. Very wise words.

I said, "Look in your own heart first. If something he does irritates you way more than is reasonable, look inside to see why this is such an emotional trigger for you."

On around the circle we went. "Put him first," Shelley said. "You won't regret it."

I leaned toward Laura. "This advice is more for us than for them, really. They don't think any of this will ever apply to them."

Laura whispered back, "They're sure their marriages are going to be different!" We giggled.

Are we crazy, I wondered, to sit here, giddy in this bubble of expectation, knowing not only how rewarding marriage can be but how unbelievably hard?

We have been through deep waters and loss and struggle and times when we did not like each other at all. We have reached out for help, we have prayed hard, and we have come out the other side still keeping our vows and believing that marriage is good.

We still love our husbands and are loved, many years in. We still laugh.

We also know that the time for caution was months ago, back when Justin had serious talks with Kayla's dad, and Chris flew to Oregon to show Stephie he really was serious about this, and Kelly decided it was time for action and asked Lisa that fateful question.

We have a lot of faith in these young women, all full of courage and good sense. Maybe you are more careful what sort of young man you choose when you know that ten aunts and your mom will ask you hard questions about his character, attitudes, faults, goals, finances, driving record, history, church, and treatment of his mom.

If you have lingering delusions about one soul mate who will always meet your heart-deep longings, as 88 percent of young Americans apparently do, those same aunts will quickly scrub that notion out of your mind.

I put the kettle on for tea and warmed the teapots. Laura melted the chocolate for the fountain. The brides began opening gifts. Jenny and Allison, the two peas-in-a-pod fourteen-year-old cousins who have already pledged to be each other's bridesmaids, begged for stories.

"Tell about when Uncle John proposed!"

Laura sighed and smiled. "OK, so we were driving along a freeway in Virginia, and all of a sudden he just turned to me and asked if I'd marry him! And there was this really noisy truck passing us right then, so I wasn't sure if I'd heard right, plus I couldn't believe he would just ask me like that, so I said, 'What did you say?' I was upset. I didn't say yes right away. I said, 'Well, I'm only eighteen. You'll have to talk to my dad.'"

The girls howled. Laura said, "For years, I just hated it when women would start telling their engagement stories. I did *not* want to tell mine."

Today, twenty-four years later, John is one of the most attentive and romantic husbands around. Laura is devoted to him, and she tells her proposal story with humor and grace.

We nibbled on pineapple wedges dipped in chocolate, sipped tea, and told of wedding-dress regrets and wedding-day fiascos and the father-in-law who refused to wear a boutonniere, not that we're still bitter about this.

Great-Aunt Alice told of her and Rick's twelve years together, all of them happy. "I can't relate to all your advice about getting along, because we never really had disagreements to work through. Rick was just that sort of man."

We nodded, still missing him.

The gifts, all new and untested, sat in three large piles. The brides posed for pictures, a triad of wisdom, innocence, and hope, endlessly smiling.

We rinsed the dishes, poured the last of the tea, and said goodbye, with a quick hug for each bride. Then we gathered our things and headed out into the storm, holding our precious wedding dresses tight, shielding them safely from the wild wind and rain.

3.

Our Forebears:

Black, Church Shoes and Four-Buckle Overshoes

Threads of Our Heritage

I was in the office checking my e-mail early on the first of May when my thirteen-year-old daughter, Jenny, wandered in with her bushy, red ponytail bouncing.

"It was hard," she said, brushing at her skirt, "because there's grass clippings on everything because the boys just mowed the yard. I got them on my face and everything."

"Hard?" I said. "What were you doing? Taking pictures?"

She grinned. "No. I was trying to wash my face in the dew."

I turned and looked at her. Brown eyes; long, unruly hair; a bridge of freckles across her nose that, as her biased mom, I think is one of the cutest sights I have ever seen.

Oh dear, surely not. "You don't like your freckles?"

She laughed. "I don't mind my freckles. I just thought it would be fun."

My mother, who is now ninety-one, had red hair and freckles back in the days when they were considered ugly. She would wash her face and arms in dew in the early morning on the first day of May in hopes that the freckles would fade and she would at last be beautiful.

I tell my children this story every year as May approaches. Three of my six inherited their grandma's coloring. I tell them how beautiful they are and how glad I am they were born in an era when red hair is no longer considered ugly.

Mom's rusty color is still there, although faded. However, she couldn't have gone out to wash in dew this year even if she wanted to because she was in the hospital with a broken hip.

When I flew to Minnesota to visit her and Dad a few weeks ago, Mom welcomed me with a typical meal of baked chicken, macaroni, homemade dinner rolls, homemade jelly, homegrown green beans, a lettuce salad, homemade applesauce, peaches from the freezer, and cookies from my brother's wife, Anna.

But Mom complained of feeling dizzy, and, less than two weeks later, a dizzy spell led to a bad fall, a broken hip, and surgery.

"She's doing very well for her age," Mom's nurse told me on the phone. "She's eating well, she's doing therapy every day, and she's in very good spirits."

Now that Mother's Day is here and I've cleared my schedule to accommodate another trip to Minnesota, I think about mothers and daughters, nieces and aunts, cousins and grandmas, and the sturdy threads that connect us and weave our lives together.

At Jenny's age, we see ourselves as unique in the universe, distinct from everyone else. When I shopped for fabric for Jenny's summer dresses, she wanted stuff I wouldn't think of wearing: zebra stripes and solid black and a shrieking yellow.

At my age, however, I see how much we share, how indistinct the lines become between ourselves and our mother, sisters, daughters.

My sister Rebecca took a picture of Mom and me shopping together. No woman likes a back-view photo of herself, but I forgave her because the photo was both striking and sweet. Mom and I are both stepping along in our solid-color jackets, long skirts, and size-eight-wide shoes. She is more stooped, but we are obviously cut from the same genetic cloth.

Mom raised three boys on a farm and made the neatest patches in jeans that I have ever seen. Others used more efficient methods, ripping out the side seam and quickly mending by machine. Mom, however, put her left hand up the pant leg, put a thimble on her right middle finger, and did it right—stitch by firm, even stitch—with a tough, gray thread.

For some reason, Mom never tried to teach me the skill or asked me to help out. But, when I had a small son, I asked Mom to teach me.

Then, like Mom, I also raised three sons and mended innumerable jean-knees.

Lately I've been intrigued with online tutorials, how-to posts in which people share step-by-step instructions, illustrated with photos, on such things as making a smooth white sauce or building a greenhouse.

Why not a tutorial on mending? I thought. Maybe others would like to learn the old-fashioned skills. So I mended an L-shaped tear in a pair of my son Steven's jeans, carefully photographing as I went.

Posting the photos and writing the directions took longer than the mending itself, I think.

A week later I went on the computer at the appointed time, plugged in the headset and enjoyed a video chat with my daughter in Jamaica.

"Oh, hey, I need to show you something," she said, and adjusted the camera so her denim skirt came on the screen. And there was a neat patch.

"I tore it on the picnic table," she said. "So I followed your tutorial and mended it."

She grinned.

So did I.

Mom would have too, I'm sure of it.

Even though Mom was hardworking and practical, she found time for stories—retelling our favorites, reading to us in the evenings. When she wasn't mending old jeans or sewing new ones, she read the Little House books, evangelistic booklets from Moody Press—like *One Little Lie . . . and Susie*—and countless others.

The next generation got lighter fare. My niece Annette posted on Facebook recently that she was reading *Bread and Jam for Frances* to a boy she baby-sits. She said, "Takes me back to being a child . . . sitting as tight as I could next to Grandma and listening as she read our favorites over and over again."

Her sister, Janet, commented, "Love this book! I found two books the other day that Grandma used to read to me. I was so happy!"

My sister chimed in, "My favorite line is, 'Sunny side-up eggs lie there and look at you in a funny way.'"

And Annette said, "I love reading classics to him. I will admit, though, that after the third time through this one in a day, I start skipping details like in what order Albert ate his lunch and Father's rant on veal cutlets. Grandma would be appalled."

Three generations of women who can quote Frances at the moment when only Frances will do—that is a very special thing.

Of course, the three generations all know the story of Mom and her freckles. We think of her washing in dew on the first of May, and it makes us sad, because to us she has always been beautiful.

On our last visit, my sister and I helped Mom into a new outfit. Rebecca had sewed a dress for her in a soft purple, with the proper cape and the old-fashioned Amish collar that Mom always wore but didn't make us put on our dresses. I got her a new sweater.

Rebecca took Mom over to the couch and leaned over and shouted at Dad, who is ninety-five. "Look at your bride! Isn't she beautiful?"

Dad, who is normally not sentimental, looked at her and smiled and said, "She has always been beautiful."

We all had tears in our eyes, including Dad.

How sturdy the fabric of our heritage is, the threads woven from Mom through me and my sisters and on to our nieces and daughters—patches and stories, food and stitches, freckles and laughter. A teenage granddaughter washes in dew on the first of May just for fun, in honor of Grandma, and knows she is also beautiful like Grandma, inside and out, her red hair and freckles glowing in the early light.

The Right Way to Tell a Story

My sister-in-law Barb was over last evening, sitting in a wing chair reading a book while we waited for the rest of the siblings to come for a family meeting.

Suddenly, I remembered something. I had a story to tell my family before everyone arrived. Nothing as profound as a family legend sort of story, nor an embarrassing experience story, but a did-you-hear-what-happened story that was worth more than just a simple statement of fact.

That is the first step—deciding if it's worthy. Even I, who can yarn a story out of accidentally sweeping the cat off the porch, admit that a few things merit only a brief sharing of information. But this called for more.

Next, I made sure I had the attention of everyone within earshot. My family laughs at me for this habit, but a story falls flat if you have to go back and repeat the first half because people were rattling dishes or reading the sports page.

"Did you hear about Katie?" I asked, sitting up straight with my eyes open wide, the universal signals for "Hear me, People, I have something to say."

"I heard she was sick," my daughter Emily said.

That was a great introduction. I wound up for the first pitch, so to speak, but just as I took a deep breath,

"She has a pancreatic cyst!" Barb burst out.

I was horrified.

"You truly are a Smucker!" I said with maybe a little more

vehemence than the situation required.

Barb looked bewildered.

"You finish my stories!" I wailed. "With the ending! Before I get there!"

Barb, I am guessing, was thinking, "What? You asked. I answered."

I have been married for almost thirty years. My husband comes from a wonderful family of generous and loving people, who take care of each other and work hard and say exactly what they think with no malice and no subtle twists and no feelings getting hurt.

I am sure a few of us in-laws have been a mystery to them, with our abundant complicated emotions and tendency toward drama, but they have always acted like this was OK and we weren't obligated to be just like them.

Like many other things, we were not a big deal. Such acceptance is a blessed relief.

So I have come to accept and even enjoy our differences, except for this one flaw—so shockingly different from how I was raised—of cutting in to finish someone's story in the most efficient way possible.

I come from Yoder-Miller-Schlabach stock, where storytelling is high art, perfected around picnic tables at family reunions, by the hitching post after an Amish Sunday service, or in a hot kitchen full of sisters-in-law and steaming applesauce.

First, the pause in the conversation, the little smile that portends a great story, the slow introduction, the expressive gesture, the heavy pause, the mimicked conversation, the building tension, the sitting up straighter, then another pause, and finally the blessed ending, followed by wild laughter or a few tears of heartfelt empathy.

The audience also knows its role well—the attentive listening, the affirming nods, the well-timed chuckle or shake of the head or murmured German *ai sis unfaschtandich,* which means anything from, "Oh my" to "You've got to be kidding" to "Shocking. Just unbelievable."

You don't interrupt the story. Everyone knows this. If you need the lemonade, you quietly gesture to Levi at the end of the table, and never in a hundred years would you do something so shameful as to speak up and give away the end of the story.

From retelling the incident in line at WinCo to the story of Great-Grandma and Aunt Kettie selling cherries in Portland, this is how it's done. It's the Right Way.

The Smuckers were not raised like this.

To them, it's all about getting to the point as quickly as possible. The facts are important, the information, and the conclusion. And, most of all, stating it immediately if you know it. They have no tolerance for waiting, for suspense. They have no compunctions about interrupting.

This is why Barb blurted out that Katie had a pancreatic cyst.

Mercifully for my precious little story, it so happened that none of my listeners had understood exactly what Barb said, so this time, for once, the story was saved. I told it from the beginning: How Katie was going along fine and then, suddenly and with no warning at all, wasn't feeling well, and her mom found her upstairs in terrible pain, and they spent the day at the hospital instead of at Courtney's graduation, and it turned out to be a cyst *this big,* and this week they'll probably do surgery.

Not the most amazing of tales, I admit, but worthy of a proper telling.

This is what you don't think about ahead of time, I want to tell the parade of happy, young couples getting married this summer: Your spouse's family, fun and supportive bunch that they might be, is in many ways a different culture from your own family.

They are going to do some things completely wrong, things that your family has always done right. Roles, communication styles, whether you fuss over a sick person or leave them alone, whether or not you eat everything you put on your plate.

Or, that's how it seems to you. Your spouse will see it from the opposite angle, with the labels reversed.

Part of what makes marriage such an amazing institution is the process of slowly mixing your cultures so you both end up better people than you would have been otherwise.

My subtle-timing, story-telling family also taught me the unfortunate communication style of turning silent and sad when I was upset, and waiting for someone else to notice and ask what's wrong.

I didn't realize how far I've come until I saw a certain daughter do the same thing the other day, all forlorn on the other side of the dinner table, waiting for us to say something.

"Listen," I said, blunt and articulate as any born-and-bred Smucker, "no more of this. You either bring it up and talk about it or be happy."

I still think it's ill-mannered to interrupt another's story and insert the ending, but my determined training of my children hasn't worked very well. The genes prevail. You must say it or die.

Some time ago my husband said, "Are you looking forward to getting together with my family next week?"

I said, "Yes, except I have to prepare myself that if I do get to tell a story and other people can actually hear me, someone else is bound to . . ."

"Finish it?" interrupted a daughter.

I gave up. This was beyond fixing.

We all laughed.

This is my message for the newlyweds: Learn from each other; bend your old ideas; flex your limits of acceptance. Some things are wrong; some are right; some are both, just from different perspectives. Love your in-laws anyhow. Let things go. Laugh a lot at the stuff that drives you crazy. It will make a great story someday, and maybe you'll get to tell it all the way to the end.

Blackberry Brockel Soup

I have become my mother, and I blame the blackberries.

Exuberantly reaching through the vines for another clump of purple berries, while also smiling indulgently at my reluctant teenage daughter, I felt the metamorphosis happening, just like that. In fact, two separate traits of Mom's had funneled down and become this moment, some thirty-five years later.

The first, of course, was Mom's love of blackberries.

We lived in the hills of southeastern Ohio for five years when I was very young. The mountain that reared up directly behind the house had some rocky fields where we tried to raise corn, but mostly it held woods full of huge maples and endless tangled blackberry bushes.

Every summer, Mom went a little crazy over those blackberries. She would put on a big straw hat, round up us children, and go tramping up the tractor lane and off into the back corners of the farm, where we picked into plastic buckets while Mom smiled a lot and didn't complain about the heat or the thorns.

Was it because they were free for the taking or that she simply loved blackberries that much? She baked them into cobblers and sprinkled them into the wonderful Amish dish known as *brockel supp* that we ate on summer evenings. It consisted of homemade white bread torn into chunks in a soup bowl, topped with lots of berries and a spoonful of sugar, then drenched in cold milk.

"Soggy bread? Really?" grimaced my sister-in-law Bonnie

when I shared this recipe. Bonnie did not grow up Amish and doesn't understand. It's one of the best foods in the universe.

The most astonishing thing about Mom's passion for blackberries is that she had to risk Ohio's many black snakes to get these berries. Far too plentiful and impossibly long and straight, like a black garden hose, these evil creatures would lie across the path and then start moving, slowly, both ends hidden for a breathtakingly long time until the tapered end finally slipped away.

Mom hated snakes and hoed to death any she found in the garden, but she didn't kill black snakes in the berry patch and seemed to see them as worth the terror they caused if she got a nice batch of berries.

Thankfully, I do not risk black snakes when I pick in Oregon, because I am almost as passionate as my intrepid mother. I sniff out the best patches by exploration and word of mouth. I climb fences and trespass on others' fields and embarrass my children and keep stopping to pick more long after the others are finished and waiting in the car.

I've expanded Mom's repertoire into blackberry cheesecake, coffee cakes and muffins. For breakfast I eat cereal and yogurt topped with berries and whipped cream.

The only difference is that I don't wear a straw hat when I pick.

The second trait of Mom's that I saw in myself that day was her belief that getting the job done was all that mattered. Hot weather and physical ailments and one's feelings might make it a little harder, but they weren't to be taken seriously. You did what you needed to do.

Mom, who was Old Order Amish for many years, didn't learn to drive a car until she was in her fifties and I was almost out of high school. I served as her chauffeur as soon as

I got my driver's license.

This worked in Mom's favor the summer she lined up a number of housecleaning jobs in town, and I not only drove her the eighteen miles to and from, but I also had to help her clean.

I hated this. I complained loudly and repeatedly. I may have been in tears a few times. It was humiliating, degrading, hot, and dirty. What if my classmates, who had glamorous summer jobs like detasseling hybrid corn, found out that I was cleaning houses with my mom? I said that if someone doesn't want to do something as badly as I didn't want to do this, surely she shouldn't have to. But I didn't have a choice.

I now find it intriguing how Mom reacted. At other times, she would set me straight with a few choice words in Pennsylvania German, but that summer she didn't. She just acted calm and amused and told me to take those fake grapes off Mrs. Wendroth's wall, bring some more hot water, and vacuum the furniture.

Mostly, she let me own my emotions without telling me I shouldn't feel that way but also without taking them too seriously.

I'm guessing we needed the money to put food on the table and gas in the car, since the farm was more loss than profit in those days. Mom knew that, but I was still in the stage of thinking a magic fairy would somehow provide.

So I worked with Mom all summer, and she let me whine all I wanted.

These two traits of hers funneled together into that episode last week when suddenly I was my mother all over again.

I would never have found those berry bushes at the edge of the field behind our Mennonite church on the outskirts of Brownsville if we hadn't held my mother-in-law's eightieth birthday party there.

We needed an outdoor spot to take pictures of the entire group. Over there the background was ugly, and over here everyone squinted in the sunshine. Finally, we found a workable spot in the grass field, shaded by the neighbor's trees. I shot the photos and turned around to find blackberry bushes with the most gorgeous clusters of wild berries I'd seen all summer. Best of all, they were easily accessible on the hard-packed edge of the field.

Some days later, I shoved a stepladder and ice-cream buckets into the car and asked my fourteen-year-old daughter to come with me to pick berries. I was bouncy and excited about this. She was not.

On the way, she said, "Do we really need to do this, don't we have enough berries, can't we just go home, and why don't you pick them yourself if you enjoy it so much?"

I said, Yes, no, no, it's twice as fast with two, and it'll be fun.

We got to church, which is normally deserted during the week. Big trucks and mysterious equipment moved into place east of the church building.

Jenny hissed, "Mom! Let's go home! There are people here!"

I said, "Oh, they'll never notice us. Here, you take the stepladder and I'll take the clippers and buckets."

Yes, I actually made her carry a stepladder past those four construction workers. My older daughter told me later that this was truly taking things too far, past basic responsibility and well into heartless cruelty.

I was sure the men never noticed us since they were busy digging up the old gravel in the children's play area with a lively little white machine.

We began picking. I exclaimed over the generous clusters. We took turns climbing the stepladder and cutting away vines so we could reach deeper into the bushes.

Jenny let me know she was not happy, and she yelled miserably when she got tangled in a long, thorny vine. I rescued her and then kept picking. It was a lovely day, and the berries hung there, smiling at me. "Right here," they said. "We've been waiting for you. We're so glad you came."

Jenny laid out her trump card. "Are these berries more important than my feelings?"

Distracted, I said, "Actually, yes." And at that moment I became my mother, irrevocably and for all time.

Jenny was quiet, convinced I was beyond help.

The next day, Jenny apologized, laughing, for her attitude. "I was just in a bad mood and everything looked so fruitless."

She wasn't trying to be clever.

I said, "It's OK. I understand," and then I apologized for being so cold-hearted, and all was well.

Jenny said she wanted to make lunch for me. I stayed out of the kitchen until she told me to come in.

With a flourish, she set a bowl in front of me—broken bread, fresh blackberries, sugar, and milk. Real brockel supp, just like Mom's, cold and sweet, with just a bit of magic in those shining, delightful berries.

Seeing the Invisible

It was always Mom's idea to go visit Charles and Mary Shelley on Sunday afternoons.

We would climb into the buggy and head west on our curvy, one-lane dirt road in the hills of southeastern Ohio, to an ancient farmhouse with huge bushes around it.

Charles and Mary, brother and sister, were of some impossibly old age. My predominant memory of their place is the pervasive darkness. I recall the house as a deep, weather-beaten gray on the outside, the paint long since peeled away. Inside, only a bit of dim light from the windows illuminated the accumulation of years.

A narrow path led through the kitchen, past the table on the left—with perhaps a dirty plate or the shriveled remains of a daffodil bouquet we had given them weeks before—and the black woodstove on the right, with mysterious piles and objects beside and behind. Then we would turn left into the living room and sit around the coal-burning stove on uncertain chairs while Mary sat in a rocking chair that had an arm fastened on with baling twine.

Everything was covered in coal dust. Anything we touched left a black smudge on our fingers, and everything we couldn't touch was obviously dusty as well—the lace curtains sagging in gloomy shreds at the dirty windows; Charles' ragged jacket; the calendars from bygone years still hanging from nails on the ancient, peeling wallpaper; the careful pile of empty Bufferin boxes on the once-lovely side table in the living room. Even Mary's little wire-rimmed glasses were so smudged and dusty we wondered how she could see through them.

With every visit, the details of that place embedded into my fascinated mind. I remember longing to explore the historic wonders in the shadowy corners. Legend had it that one door in the living room led to a parlor with an organ and another door led upstairs to heaven-only-knew what treasures. But any curiosity on our part was quickly squelched by a glare from Mom, who sensed Mary's nervousness when we wandered too far or poked too deep.

My brother Fred managed to leave the conversation one afternoon and walk softly into the kitchen. He was inspecting the old woodstove when suddenly a rooster crowed loudly, right beside him it seemed, and Fred was so startled he whacked his head on the overhanging pie-warmer.

Charles and Mary had felt sorry for their pet rooster out in the cold weather, and had placed him in a wooden crate in the kitchen.

So we would try to sit quietly and contain our curiosity while Charles and Mary told Mom and Dad about the old days and Charlie's last visit to the doctor and if they were staying warm this winter and that they were thinking about maybe getting a telephone and how soon they predicted the bush outside, that their mother had planted, would bloom with its unusual, fragrant, coral-colored blossoms.

We left Ohio and moved to Minnesota when I was ten. As I recall, other neighbors kept us informed, now and then, as the Shelleys grew older and eventually passed away. In the forty years since, I have never met anyone quite like Charles and Mary.

Which says a lot about my mother.

Mom passed away suddenly last month at the age of ninety-three. My family traveled to Minnesota, where snow drifted deeply across the dirt roads, fierce winds blew, and the temperature dropped below zero the day of the funeral and burial.

Mom would not have thought the weather was such a big deal, as she almost never let ice and snow stop her from anything.

And she would not have appreciated that her funeral turned into such a big fuss, with people stranded at airports, cars stuck in snowdrifts, and many worried phone calls, all for her sake.

Among the family, publicly at her service, and around the tables at the dinner that followed, our stories repeatedly circled back to what a remarkable person she was.

Mom raked leaves and washed windows well past the age of ninety. She quilted and sewed and crocheted, hauled and hoed and cooked and canned.

She got enormous enjoyment from watching animals out her windows and detailing their activities in letters to her large family. The deer and pheasants were browsing in the cornfield every morning, she would report. The rooster thinks the feisty, old cat with one ear is his girlfriend, she wrote me once. They hang out together every day in front of the barn.

She trapped skunks in the old silo in a Havahart Trap and killed rats in the garage. She made exquisite jellies and blessed her children with handmade rugs and quilts.

But, always, our stories came back to Mom and her astonishing gift for noticing people. Unlike the rest of us, who often charge through life ignoring most people and taking note only of important ones who have something to offer us, Mom saw individual people with a sharp clarity, wise insight, and heartfelt concern.

Mom gave birthday cards to children and plates of cookies to the "old people" at church, who eventually were all younger than she and Dad.

She hunted through the Amish newspaper, *The Budget*, for news of people who were sick or injured, and she sent them get-well cards or homemade scrapbooks with Bible verses and illustrations. "Here is a shower announced," she would say, and we knew a card and letter would soon be in the mail.

She worried about teenagers who seemed to be struggling and made a point of trying to encourage them.

Even in the nursing home in recent months, fuzzy with dementia, she would sit in the lounge, watch people, and murmur her observations. "That man over there, now, he is someone who would help you if you needed it." Of a small and energetic activities director, she whispered, "That little goose. She thinks she's so smart!"

Mostly, though, we marveled at how Mom took note of the invisible people. In any crowd, Mom would locate the loneliest outcast and start a conversation. If you were dirty, poor, or eccentric, Mom was your friend. If you were toothless and cussed a bit, so much the better. If you were the sort that everyone walked by without seeing, Mom would not only see you but shake your hand and ask about your arthritis.

If you served anonymously behind the scenes, she searched you out, thanked you, and made you a pan of cinnamon rolls for Christmas.

And if you were isolated from the rest of society, like Charles and Mary Shelley, she found you, visited you on Sunday afternoons, and made sure you stayed warm in winter.

I don't think it ever crossed her mind that people might not quite know what to make of this friendly Amish woman. She didn't worry about appearances, or association, or what important people might think.

In the fifth grade and new to public school, I made the mistake of telling Mom about a girl named Carmen in the fourth grade who always looked sad and dirty.

Even though Mom had never met her, Carmen became her project. I was supposed to talk with her and be her friend. My protests that we were in different rooms made no difference. We passed on the stairs, didn't we? "All right. You can be nice to her then."

I didn't try telling Mom my biggest concern, that it would not be cool to be Carmen's friend. I wasn't that stupid.

That spring, Mom's sister gave her a lavender homemade candle shaped like an enormous egg. Mom had a brilliant idea—I was to give this to Carmen, to show her that somebody cared about her! I kept silent about the fact that this was a terrible idea in every direction, and I meekly carried the heavy candle, wrapped in tissue paper, to school, where I mercifully found Carmen alone for the moment and gave her the candle.

To Mom's joy, she met Carmen in the laundromat downtown not long afterward, recognizing her from my descriptions. "Did Dorcas give you a candle?" she asked.

Carmen actually smiled a little, Mom reported later, and then Carmen said, "Yes, and it looks like an egg."

You would have thought Mom had won a new kitchen, she was so pleased.

During the hard transitions of her life, Mom always turned to sewing. These days, since her passing, I find myself doing the same. I sew dresses for my daughters and run my hands over my stash of cotton scraps, planning projects like Mom's that are useful and resourceful and economical.

Mostly, though, I think not so much about sewing or even about missing Mom but about having eyes that really see. I wonder how one receives that rare vision that focuses not only on projects and deadlines and prominent people, but on the dirty, the invisible, the outcast, the dusty and lonely treasures down a hidden gravel road.

Long Term Investments

It's a strange, separate world in the intensive care unit.
Wires and tubes snake out from under ugly gowns, luminous green lines trace mountainous paths over computer screens, and odd machines whoosh and whir like living things.

My mother-in-law, Anne, had seemed like she had only a miserable case of the flu. Most people with pneumonia this bad, the doctor said, would have been turning blue at the edges, coughing up blood, and hardly breathing for pain. So she wasn't diagnosed until the pneumonia was life-threatening, and she was in the ICU for days on end until she finally transitioned to a regular room, once again breathing on her own.

"We can't leave her alone," said Rosie, the youngest of the seven siblings, that first afternoon. "She wouldn't have left us alone when we were little."

Rosie, like all the others, speaks bluntly, sees clearly, and does what she needs to do.

All right, then.

My husband, Paul, Anne's second child and the expert planner in a family of organizers, helped with scheduling: This one in the morning; Lois during the day; a son after work; another one after dinner; maybe an in-law overnight.

I took my shift on a Tuesday night, hauling a pillow, snacks, and magazines and missionary newsletters to read. I slipped through the double doors into that bright, alien world of beeping gauges and uncomfortable chairs, of rolling machines that probably cost as much as a new car, and a simple handwritten sign that read: SPEAK INTO LEFT EAR.

Ever-present, of course, was that deep-down worry and those constant silent prayers. Please, please, hear us; have mercy.

One's thoughts go in many directions in the ICU at night, from death and life to dinner tomorrow, past and future, and is it morning yet, and our choices and our stories and how they will all turn out.

I took my turn with Anne a number of times that week. The ICU staff seemed a bit overwhelmed with Smuckers. "We put her on the machine earlier when John was here," the nurse told me. "Or wait, maybe it was Paul. Or Steve? Is there a Steve?"

"Yes," I said. "And Lois and Rosie. And everyone's spouses. And two more siblings arriving this weekend."

We had been coming in ones and twos, according to ICU rules, and the grandchildren hadn't even been there. If Anne got moved to a regular room, I figured, we'd descend in such swarms as the nurses had never seen.

While I took my turn in the stiff, vinyl chair, listening to Anne's breathing, with too much time to think, I always circled back to motherhood as an act of faith. A woman has babies and invests her life in them without knowing the outcome, working and loving and giving for an unknown future.

"And now these three remain: faith, hope and love," says the writer of the Bible's famous "love chapter." He concludes: "But the greatest of these is love."

Love may be the greatest, but I think mothers need large and equal portions of faith and hope as well.

I thought of my six and their progress through the years. For the girls: the giggle years, the horse years, the fashion years. For the boys: the filthy years, the football years, the fighting years.

Love gets you through the moment, empowering you to reach through impossible fatigue or frustration to clean the vomit or settle the fight or make another lunch.

But faith and hope give perspective: Surely this will all pay off one day in adults who do what needs to be done without being told—a deep belief to ward off the fears that at thirty they will still fight over who rides "shotgun."

Anne is not one to dramatize the past. Her life with small children seems to have faded into a hazy, happy memory, but I know it couldn't have been easy. Seven children in about fourteen years, and each child full of noise and personality and outspoken opinions, with lots of red hair and freckles in the mix, living together in a small house.

My husband tells of riding in someone's car when he was maybe ten years old. He closed the door—not extra hard, he thought—and part of the door handle broke off in his hand. The driver snapped, "You Smuckers! You always break everything!"

That story told me a lot.

What kept Anne going? I wondered. What mix of love and hope and faith kept her cooking and teaching and bandaging and cleaning for that crew? What kept her believing it would all turn out well? Because, in the end, it did.

Here she was, seventy-nine and sick, and a stream of tall, grown-up, responsible adults showed up at their appointed times, coming when they were expected, sitting quietly with her until the next sibling arrived, fetching anything she needed.

I thought, suddenly, *This, right here—this is where it all comes together for a mother.* All those babies you had and got up nights with and thought would never grow up. And you wondered in dark moments if you were pouring out your life for nothing, if your investment would ever pay off.

Well, it does. It pays off in these sons and daughters who come and go and do not leave you alone in the hospital. If all the other benefits of children were not considered, this in itself would be worth it—that in this dark time of advancing age and helpless illness, they pause their busy lives and return the life you poured into them.

On a Saturday afternoon, the seven siblings and most of the spouses, plus a grandchild or two, gathered around Anne's bed, now in a normal hospital room, and sang the old family favorites: "I Cannot Come," "Neither Do I Condemn Thee," and more. Their voices meshed in that smooth way that only family members' voices can blend, especially if they're talented to start with and learned to sing together as children.

Anne, propped up in her bed, listened with tearful eyes and a smile. "It's like a taste of heaven," she said.

These days, Anne is back on her feet and breathing well. She will soon move in with Rosie's family in the room they built with her in mind.

She does not think in grand terms of life coming full circle and all her investments paying off. She is just happy to be cared for.

Looking on, I am happy to see that, for this mother at least, faith and hope were fulfilled, love was rewarded, and life turned out exactly like it ought to.

Silly Stories and Squished Berries

We went to pick strawberries an hour after we got home from Minnesota, even though the van was still stuffed to the rafters with the old pie safe and Grandpa Adam's little table and the Formica® cutting board shaped like a pig that my uncle once made for Mom.

As we rolled heavily down Interstate 84, with Mount Hood ahead, more than twenty hours of driving behind us, and our son Steven nonchalantly at the wheel, my husband called our friend TJ of Bear Fruit to see if the berries were still available.

"My wife is desperate," he said. "We've been in Minnesota for her dad's sale, and she's afraid she's going to miss out on the strawberries."

Paul got off the phone. "They still have plenty. They're not as big, but we can still get them."

Yes!

We turned into our driveway at 3:30 p.m., cleaned up a bit, looked at the mail, and drove to the patch, where TJ's wife, Marcia, gave us buckets and directed us to the pink flags.

Green leaves pushed aside, bright-red berries underneath, sun shining, dirt under my knees, family near me. The first bite was a taste of heaven.

Everything was going to be all right.

In Minnesota strawberries ripen at the end of June, and when I was a child, the nearest U-pick patch was almost an hour away. Once a year, we would rise early, Mom and my sisters, Rebecca and Margaret, and me, and load the car with ice-cream buckets and huge stainless-steel bowls.

The routine never varied.

First, we picked with excitement, tasting frequently.

Then we picked efficiently, marveling at the clusters of red down under the overhanging green.

Hours passed, and buckets filled. Mom picked steadily, crouching in her worn dress and apron, with a bandana on her head.

Margaret inevitably got us started throwing rotten berries at each other. We giggled about the people in the next row and ate far too many berries without considering their high moisture content.

We talked with other pickers about the quality of the berries and the weather and also about us, since this was far enough from home that people weren't used to our "plain" appearance.

"Are you sisters?" an older woman in the next row once asked us.

"Yes, we are."

"What order are you with?"

"Order?"

A confused conversation followed until we figured out that she meant Catholic nuns and we meant female siblings.

By the time Mom finally decided we had picked enough, the sun was high and hot, we were dirty and tired and hungry, and our fingers were stained red.

We trekked down the long rows carrying our overflowing buckets, which we piled on the table in front of the little shed. While the cashier weighed and Mom paid, we girls dashed to the nearby Porta-Potty and danced desperately as we waited in line, the same urgency—due to the same indulgence—having afflicted many of the pickers at once.

We drove home, knowing that our work was far from finished.

After a quick lunch, we sat around the kitchen table and stemmed berries for the rest of the day. Mom washed and cut and sugared. We scooped them into square containers for the freezer.

By late afternoon, our fingers ached and we were tired of strawberries. Descending into silliness, we laughed crazily at things that weren't that funny. We quit eating berries.

I recall once dropping an overripe berry down Rebecca's back and squishing it flat.

Finally, we were finished. Stacks of containers carried to the freezer, clanking bowls sloshed in the sink, stems tossed to the pigs, and then we could scatter to relax and read a book or go outside to sit under a tree and just breathe.

Selling your parents' belongings, moving your dad into your brother's basement apartment next door, and saying goodbye to the home place is like a berry-picking day on a much larger scale.

We assembled the family, dove in with enthusiasm, worked impossibly hard, descended into silliness, exhausted ourselves beyond bearing, and were so sick of the stuff at hand—in this case, old papers and glass jars and Cool Whip containers—that we never wanted to see them again.

Mom and Dad sold their farm in 1984, the summer Paul and I got married, and moved onto a five-acre property half a mile up the road. Sadly, the house and many heirlooms burned in 1987, but they rebuilt on the same site.

So, for thirty years of our marriage, that was the place we went home to.

From Highway 4 we would turn onto the dirt road. A mile west and the road stopped at a T with another gravel road, but we would continue straight ahead, down the long driveway with neighbor Olaf Johnson's crops on the left, around the awkward uphill curve, and then we were there: red barn with goats and cats and a pig or steer, the shed with the old Farmall tractor, and the white house with Mom rushing out to hug us.

We had big Christmas dinners there, and birthday parties, and lots of coffee. We came with our babies, and Mom took care of both them and us, insisting that we needed a break. She made Popsicles for the grandchildren that they ate on the deck on summer evenings. She cut fresh lettuce from the garden and showed us all her latest quilts.

None of us liked to sleep in the basement bedroom under the kitchen because Dad was always up before 6:00 a.m., marching back and forth across the kitchen in his hard-soled shoes, fixing his oatmeal with its secret added ingredients, and brewing his mysterious hot drink that kept him healthy these ninety-seven years.

Did it really take that many trips across the kitchen to accomplish this, we wondered, stuffing our heads under pillows and feeling like the troll beneath the bridge, with Papa Billy Goat Gruff trip-trapping over our heads.

Dad's morning routine never changed, but other things did. The corners got dirty, the basement smelled funny, and dark things accumulated in the garage.

When we came home, we took care of Mom instead of she taking care of us.

Mom and Dad were determined to stay in the house and remain fully independent until they died. We all worked together to make it possible, and they stayed until Mom broke another hip and was overcome by dementia.

She passed away last December. Dad realized that the heart and life of the house was gone and said he was ready to sell and move out.

So we came from Oregon; Oklahoma; Washington, DC; and Pennsylvania. From Turkey and Yemen and Canada.

We dug and sorted and washed and boxed and recycled and threw away.

We told stories and laughed until tears ran down our cheeks, especially when Anna, a sister-in-law, described the frightening experience of coming upon Dad suited up with goggles, mask, and gloves to spray his apple trees. Rebecca found the old enema apparatus that Mom, having trained as a nurse in the 1940s, relied on to bring down fevers, which taught us quickly that it behooved us to stay healthy.

We found forgotten teacups and old report cards and an unexplained box labeled "Letters—Discouraging Times."

And then, exhausted, we sold what we could to friendly neighbors, sent the goats to a new owner, packed our vans, and stripped the beds. Late the last evening, Margaret's children and mine cleaned the bathrooms for the last time.

When we left, driving east on that long lane, we left empty rooms behind us, a silent barn, and an abandoned garden.

I posted a nostalgic update online, and our son Matt commented, "One era ends, another begins . . . Your house is quickly becoming 'the home to go back to' for your children."

Today we picked more strawberries, pushing the season's deadline. The children are busy stemming, talking, getting tired, and growing gradually more silly.

I hope to have fifty pints in the freezer by the end of the day, all washed and cut and sugared—a big job accomplished because we worked together until it was done, because this is what families do, and this is how a home is made.

Grandma and the Media

Some time ago, my daughter looked up from the book she was reading and asked, "Mom, what was the Iron Curtain?"

I tried to convey to her not only the facts about the border between the Communist world and the free world but also the enormous fears I felt at her age, when I heard the words Iron Curtain. At school, we often discussed the latest tensions in US-Soviet relations and the possibility of nuclear war. At prayer meeting, we faithfully prayed for the Christians "behind the Iron Curtain" who were being persecuted for their faith.

Back then, I always thought it was almost inevitable that Communism would come to America by the time I was in my thirties, and I, too, would endure prison and torture for what I believed.

I don't think my daughter really understood. She, however, has her own set of fears. One day we were driving to a school function when we heard the news of yet another school shooting. It triggered a barrage of questions. "Was anyone killed? Why do people do that? What happens to children who shoot other children?"

I sensed in her voice a tinge of the same fears that I felt as a child. "What if this terrible thing came here, into my world?"

Obviously, school shootings can erupt close to home. In their own way, so can other troubling things in today's headlines: terrorism, wars, poverty, crime, and strained relations with other countries.

But equally troubling, I think, are media that exploit tragedy and inflame our fears but fail to provide balance with all the good things happening in the world.

For that kind of information, I suppose you need *The Budget*, a thirty-two-page newspaper published in Ohio. Described in a *New York Times* article as "The most serene escape imaginable from the news plied elsewhere," *The Budget* is filled with columns submitted by *"Budget* scribes" from Amish and Mennonite communities all over the United States and Canada. It came to our mailbox every week when I was a child, bringing news of crops, weather, new babies, and baptisms.

My mom always credited *The Budget* with improving Grandma's reading. Grandma could read and write surprisingly well considering the fact that she had attended school for only three years and was much more comfortable with German than with English. Mom was sure that it was because she read The Budget from front to back every week.

I remember Grandma reading *The Budget* at the kitchen table, translating the news into German, and adding her own commentary.

"I see here that Henry and Mattie Bender's son Chris is getting married in Indiana. Now wasn't Henry a son of Jonas Swartzentruber's first wife's brother that used to live out by the cheese factory in Kalona?"

It took Grandma a long time to read through *The Budget*.

Grandma was strong in her opinions, with no patience for foolishness, but with a wonderful sense of humor. Her strongest German adjective was unfaschtandich, which literally translates "senseless," I believe, but with Grandma's inflections it implied "totally obnoxious and disgusting." You didn't want Grandma to fix her gaze on you and say you were unfaschtandich.

One time Grandma attempted to read a newspaper besides The Budget, and that incident is instructive for us when the headlines seem especially troubling.

It was probably in the late 1960s. Grandma was approaching eighty and exhibiting signs of Alzheimer's. One summer morning, while visiting my uncle's family in Ohio, she picked up the newspaper and saw a headline: "John Lennon Says the Beatles Are 'More Popular Than Jesus.'"

A devout Christian, Grandma was upset. She took the paper to my cousin Sara and asked her what it meant. Sara explained that the Beatles were a group of men who played instruments and sang, and people liked them so much that one of these men claimed that they were more popular than Jesus.

Grandma was horrified. What was the world coming to? She muttered about it for the rest of the morning.

That afternoon, my uncle's family took Grandma to visit some friends: three older, unmarried sisters who lived down the street.

As Grandma and the others sat in the living room talking, one of the women bustled in the back door with an armload of laundry. "These awful Japanese beetles!" she exclaimed. "They crawl all over the things on the clothesline and spit on them!"

Grandma almost exploded. "Did you *hear* that?" she sputtered. "Those unfaschtandich Beatles! Not only do they say they're more popular than Jesus, but they have the nerve to go into people's backyards and spit on the clean laundry hanging on the line!"

Sara's attempts to clarify and explain proved useless, and for the rest of the day, Grandma snagged anyone who would listen and told them all about those unfaschtandich Beatles.

Grandma died in 1977. Both the Beatles and the Soviet Union disbanded long ago. The daily newspaper still has troubling headlines, and *The Budget* still doesn't. Jesus is still awfully popular, and I am still free to believe in Him. I like to think that Grandma, in heaven, would assure me if she could that many of our fears will never materialize and that things are not always what they seem to be.

Writing the Family Stories

If my husband's great-aunt Berniece hadn't written it down, who but a few aunts would remember how the family ended up on this spread of farmland along Muddy Creek and how a girl from Switzerland became my children's great-great-great grandma?

The little blue booklet, with a hand-drawn sketch of a peasant girl in high-top shoes on the cover, is held together with a simple, plastic binding, which shows that preserving the family stories doesn't need to be costly or complicated.

Memories of Mary: The Swiss Maid Who Became My Grandmother, the title reads. I picked it off my to-read stack of books just before my fifty-second birthday, and right there on the first page it said, "Mary Werner Hostetler—June 29, 1864–April 11, 1945. She was exactly ninety-eight years older than I am.

Mary's father died when she was six months old, and her grandfather took on the difficult role of providing for the widow and her four children. In 1871, they followed a relative to America, where life was better but still hard enough that Mary had to work for another family to earn her room and board.

That family happened to be Mennonite, and Mary was baptized into the church at age thirteen. She married a Mennonite man from Missouri named Joseph Hostetler, and in 1895, they moved to Oregon, north of Salem. In 1911, they moved to this area. "One mile from Harrisburg," the book says, adding, "Later, they bought some land across the road and built a better house and moved there."

I wish Berniece had added maps.

The seventy-eight pages include stories from Mary's daughters and a dozen other descendants. Mary became a well-known and respected woman who was called on often to care for the sick, deliver babies, and prepare the deceased for burial.

In other chapters we learn that Mary's grandson Herman broke his arm four times, Lloyd and his brothers made "the first self-propelled windrower ever built" out of a 1931 Chevrolet truck motor and frame turned backwards, and Berniece didn't have a name until she was four years old.

"The single most important thing you can do for your family may be the simplest of all: Develop a strong family narrative," writes Bruce Feiler in a *New York Times* article called "The Stories That Bind Us."

Feiler cites a study: "The more children knew about their family's history, the stronger their sense of control over their lives, the higher their self-esteem and the more successfully they believed their families functioned."

Stories told orally are the most entertaining, with dramatic aunts' expert timing and emphatic descriptions. But oral tales die out with the tellers, and only the most persistent stories survive.

Also, spoken stories change in the telling, but a story on paper is a fixed reference. One family legend that every child in the vast relation knows is how Great-Grandpa Daniel's life was threatened by a carload of rough young men because he refused to buy war bonds, but then his attackers suddenly left. Years later, they told of a mysterious someone keeping them from carrying out their plans.

My fifteen-year-old daughter Jenny decided to write a poem about this event for a contest, and she used Berniece's book to review the facts. She learned that three men, at three different houses, all faced the same threats.

Daniel's son Frank's chapter relates, "Only a few years ago, I found out why they didn't carry out their plans. They were prepared and ready to tar and feather us, but when they came, there was a heavenly being that stood between them and us and they couldn't get ahold of anybody. It happened at all three places."

Jenny's poem won fourth place out of eighty-seven entries. I imagine her poem tucked into the back of her grandchildren's copies of the little blue booklet.

A written record is also valuable because not everyone is a storyteller. While reading *Memories of Mary*, I was shocked to realize that if we depended entirely on my husband passing on his family history, our children would know only a tiny slice of it. He is great at passing along the values but less adept at repeating the tales.

Also, books are not limited by distance. Great-grandchildren on the other side of the country, far from the aunts and family reunions, can have the same stories easily at hand.

We have this record only because Berniece, the youngest of a large family, recognized the value of recording the family history and decided it was her job to make it happen.

Berniece interviewed her elders, wrote it down, and typed it up. She prodded siblings into sharing memories, transcribed tapes, edited a lot, and found a printer. She got a nephew's wife to draw the cover illustration, then bought multiple copies and passed them out for years, even to shirt-tail relations like me.

When you are young and your parents are healthy and your children are babies, you don't think about writing things down, beyond jotting on the calendar when little Amy started walking and the cute phrases Ben said.

But everything changes when parents are suddenly elderly. You remember a vague image from a long-ago tale and ask your mom about it. "What was that story about the time Grandma took you and Ervin on the train to visit Aunt Kitty in Cleveland? Who was Aunt Kitty? And do I remember right that Grandma wore a big hat?"

"How's that?" says your mother, once a fountain of stories. "Aunt Kitty?"

That's when you frantically start to write down all that you remember, asking your siblings, writing to aunts and uncles. "Was 'Mommie Schlabach' a twin?" "Who gave Mom that little table in the bedroom?"

Every scrap of information becomes valuable, every written word, the tiny spidery script on adhesive tape on the back of a bowl from Grandma Yoder: "For Amos. 1946."

Amos is my dad, and this summer he is working on his memoirs. In Oregon for an extended visit, he sits on the couch and writes, careful Palmer method on the back of papers advertising an odor remover.

Some people choose to type their stories, tell them to a rapidly typing grandchild, or even put on a headset and speak into an Audacity recording program on a computer.

But Dad is ninety-seven and prefers to write his history like he has always written letters—by hand, on his lap.

Dad loses his pen. I replace it. He misplaces his glasses. A kind soul finds them under a pew at church and drops them off at our house. I bring him cups of hot water, his favorite beverage. I praise what he's written and stay quiet when he's concentrating.

I pray, "Let him get it all down. Please, let his mind stay sharp, let the words form and flow into his hand and out onto the paper. Let them make sentences, paragraphs, chapters."

"Let him tell his story."

He has covered his childhood, the history of the Amish church in Oklahoma, and his Civilian Public Service days.

His grandparents lived in Mississippi, but the Amish group left because of tragedy—the young women would get sick and die in their first pregnancy. Malaria, people guessed.

His mother survived only by the grace of God, he writes. Then they moved to a safer climate in Oklahoma.

The Amish young people in his day had problems, he continues, because the young men liked to have fast horses and decorate the manes with shiny red and blue rings. The girls liked patent-leather shoes and fancy dresses.

I smile. "Oh, Dad!"

Civilian Public Service changed his life. He went from being on the farm and going to town maybe twice a year, to living in other states with a group of conscientious objectors, working on dairy farms, planting trees, and seeing the wider world for five challenging years.

At times he uses outdated terms now considered inappropriate or even racist.

"My best friend in school was an Indian boy named Woodrow Wilson." I don't tell him to use the term "Native American" instead, knowing that his heart appreciates all kinds of people and fearing that I would stop the creative flow.

He is a perfectionist, writing and rewriting. "Rough draft" he notes in a box at the top of the page.

"Just get it down," I tell him. "We can edit it later."

My daughters type up the chapters as he finishes them. Jenny reads slowly. Emily types.

"Nah vos ich neksht schrava vill, sell muss ich decida druff," he says in his German dialect when he finishes the chapter on Oklahoma. "I need to decide what to write about next."

"Your marriage," I suggest. "And your children. College. All the places you lived."

He nods, thinking. I leave quietly, and he picks up his pen and a new sheet of paper.

Slowly and deliberately, he writes. It's as though he is digging up a treasure, handing it to us for safekeeping, passing it on, word by careful word.

"He needs another day," I pray. "Strength and clarity, words and sentences."

Because we are not finished yet; our children's children need to hear this; and there is always more story to tell.

4.

Travel:

Steps on
Faraway Soil

A Day with Silent Babies

Twenty bare cribs in one room; a wet baby in each. None of them had a toy, a blanket, or a stuffed animal.

My daughters and I were the only other people in the room.

It was quiet—that was the most bizarre thing. The only noise was from the grainy TV in the corner, with a smiling couple advertising orange juice.

I reached for the nearest baby. "You might want to wait until they're bathed and dry," said my daughter Amy. "Someone should be in soon to do that."

I ignored her and picked a small blanket from a pile. I held it around a soaked baby, lifted him up, and settled in a chair.

He snuggled against me as though I were his grandma come at last.

The other babies stood in their cribs and watched enviously.

A worker bustled into the room, grabbed a stack of clean sheets from a cupboard, snatched the blanket off my lap and rushed out. The silent babies watched her.

I put the baby back in the crib so another one could have a turn, and, for the first time, the silence was broken as the baby burst into heart-rending wails.

Jenny, my youngest, watched as well. *Was this a noble idea gone a bit crazy?* I wondered, exposing a twelve-year-old American to this side of the universe, where life could be bleak beyond imagining and anything you did about it wasn't nearly enough?

It had seemed like a good idea when we first discussed it, back in Oregon.

Amy, our oldest daughter, is spending a year working at a small mission in Jamaica. She teaches the administrator's children, does the bookkeeping, and helps out with the five little foster children who were taken in from the local government-sponsored "childcare center"—essentially an orphanage—where Amy and the other workers also volunteer several days a week.

Amy hoped her dad and I could come visit her, but Paul, working two jobs and planning two other trips before harvest, didn't see how he could get away.

He had an idea.

"You haven't taken Jenny on her 'Twelve Trip' yet, have you?" he said, referring to the family tradition of my taking each child on an excursion around age twelve. "Maybe the two of you should go visit Amy."

Jenny loved the idea, but first I sent an e-mail to all the older children. This would be far fancier than any of their trips, I told them, and I didn't want the unfairness of this brought up at my funeral.

They all assured me it would be OK.

So we left an Oregon February for a week in paradise.

Like so many third-world countries, Jamaica is a land of jarring contrasts.

Famous white beaches and a friendly laid-back populace draw thousands of tourists, many of them arriving on enormous cruise ships that light up the water at night like beautiful, glowing islands.

But far from the gleaming shopping strips, gang activity has driven the murder rate to the third-highest in the world, and 85 percent of the babies are born to single mothers.

With Amy as our guide, we slathered on SPF 50 sunscreen,

swam in the turquoise Caribbean, and hiked six hundred feet up a waterfall.

We drank a grapefruit soda called Ting and ate jerk chicken in breezy open-air restaurants. Jenny played football with her new friends, admired exotic bugs, and screamed when she found a huge frog sitting in the toilet. She gave wagon rides to the little kids at the mission and swam with them in the pool.

And we spent that one day volunteering at the orphanage. After I had held about five babies, someone shooed us out of the baby room and on to our next assignment of dressing two dozen toddlers and then supervising their morning playtime.

Nonverbal, the children either screamed or kept too quiet as they maneuvered the large, battered plastic toys.

They were not given any small objects or toys to play with, so they endlessly fought over the two pairs of shoes inexplicably doled out that morning, desperate to have something small enough to hold and manipulate in their hands.

I held toddlers on my lap, two at a time, until my legs ached and my clothes were smudged with pee and dirt and snot and spit. And still they climbed all over me—eager, clinging, patting, touching, hungry for affection, screaming when I had to set them down.

"It looks like our job is to keep them from killing each other," Jenny said matter-of-factly, and she gently pulled warring children apart, gave piggyback rides, and rocked the little plastic seesaws after setting a toddler on each end.

Amy did a little of everything—holding these, playing with those, distracting others from pounding heads and pulling hair.

Among this bunch of adorable children, acceptably clean and fed but raised without attention or affection, I felt a horror and grief I could hardly contain.

Yet at the same time, watching my daughters' kindness to these emotionally abandoned children, I felt an enormous sense of accomplishment.

Raising a child is not an easy assignment, and to a long list of goals for our six we have added this: to be aware, despite the safety and plenty in which they grew up, that others in the world are far less privileged, and they should do something about it.

On a warm evening, I sat in an Adirondack chair and looked out over the city. It was like a bit of heaven, but I kept thinking of my favorite little boy at the orphanage who, even now, I knew was still there, lying in his bare crib.

Tomorrow he would be hustled from one regimented activity to the next like a well-programmed little robot, and there wasn't anything I could do about it.

Is it possible, I wondered, to fully enjoy my blessings yet be just as fully aware of the unfortunate, to live somewhere between the self-indulgent mentality of so many tourists and the asceticism of folks who can't enjoy a good cup of coffee without feeling guilty?

Amy, who knows the name not only of every child at the orphanage but also the best local restaurants, seems to have found a healthy balance. Would Jenny be able to find the same balance as she grew up?

I have reason to hope so, judging from how she plunged wholeheartedly into everything her week in Jamaica offered. With equal eagerness, she fed a plop of cooked orange squash to an orphan child in a high chair; took pictures of a huge, green bug on her arm; pushed little kids on swings; enjoyed her big sister; and ate lavish ice cream cones from the store downtown.

The night before we left, she cried, wishing we could stay longer.

Sadly, we couldn't.

But this is what I learned from her, my fearless youngest, on my final Twelve Trip: Fully enjoy what you have; fully do what you can. You can't do everything, but you can do something, and, even if it isn't much, it matters.

At least for that day. At least in that place. At least to that child.

Faith and Culture and a Laundry Lady

I hope my son's athletic pants and jeans enjoyed those three weeks in June, because I doubt they will ever be ironed again.

I think the laundry lady was my favorite thing in Thailand. Her name was Mae Wan, but among ourselves we called her Mrs. Tiggy-Winkle, after the capable little hedgehog in the Beatrix Potter book who took in laundry and was "an excellent clear-starcher."

Mae Wan was bigger than a hedgehog, but not by much, and her little shop was about a block down from our apartment, just off a busy street in Chiang Mai.

Three times a week I assembled our clothes, towels, and sheets—but not undergarments, as that's extremely rude in that culture—into two baskets, called our teenage son to help me, and set off.

In the short walk to Mae Wan's, we passed a few small shops, undersized Asian motorbikes by the dozen, and three displays of potted plants and oversized bird baths containing little lily ponds.

We always kicked off our sandals by the front door then stepped inside, where the strong scent of detergent hung in the steamy air, an iron hissed in the background, and stiffly pressed clothes hung on long bars along the wall.

Mae Wan greeted us with a delighted smile. *"Sawat dee ka"* she said, pressing her hands together and bowing slightly, and we did likewise.

Then she dumped our things into her baskets, wrote mysterious numbers on our page in her account book, and sawat dee ka'd again, sometimes with a "God bless you" in English as we slipped our sandals on and left.

The next morning we would return, and Mae Wan would greet us like we were her favorite customers. First, she handed us plastic bags with carefully pressed T-shirts and athletic pants and sheets. Then she stood on a little stool and lifted down shirts and dresses, pressed as they had never been pressed in their lives, from the bar along the wall.

I always thanked her enthusiastically. We carried our things back to our apartment while I gushed about how glorious this was and how Mae Wan made me feel like I was the queen, living in luxury. For this experience she charged only ten baht, or about thirty-three cents, per garment. I worried about taking advantage of her until I found out that for ten baht she could go around the corner and buy a nice lunch of rice and chicken.

We were in Thailand for three weeks—Paul and I and our two youngest children, seventeen-year-old Steven and thirteen-year-old Jenny—at a Mennonite Bible school founded five years earlier on the premise that if you feel called to Christian missions, you should get your training where the fewest Christians live. The school draws young people from the United States and Canada and sends them out to various points in Southeast Asia and as far as India.

Paul taught History of Missions, discussing Hudson Taylor, who shocked his British co-workers by suggesting that missionaries to China should dress, live, and talk like the Chinese; David Livingstone, who was better at exploring than preaching; and a long list of men and women who wrestled with dilemmas of how to share their faith with people in other places and cultures.

With no assigned duties, I took a Principles of Teaching class; delved into local tourist attractions; tried to keep the children occupied; cleaned our funny, narrow, four-story apartment; took laundry to Mae Wan's; learned about the culture; and pondered the questions you seldom encounter if you never travel far from your home in Harrisburg.

The paradoxes, for example: The Thai people are so deeply respectful of others that perfect strangers get smiles and bows, almost no one honks on the busy highways, and the elderly are revered to a degree that seems astonishing to Americans. Yet this same culture seems to have no respect for its young women, especially the poor from the hill tribes, who are funneled into Thailand's famous sex trade by a complex web of social, economic, and religious pressures.

No matter how many questions I asked about this, it never made sense to me.

American society is no less perplexing when viewed from across the Pacific. We tell young women they are valuable, and we encourage them to develop their talents, get an education, and contribute equally to society. Yet it was Americans who were responsible for Thailand's reputation as a destination for sex tourism, developed when soldiers traveled there for R&R during the Vietnam War.

To what degree, I wondered, is it right to judge another culture's traditions and values? What is true universally, and what is, as Americans like to say, "only true for you"? How does Christian mission work fit into Buddhist and animist Southeast Asia? When is it an imposition or coercion, and when is it offering a much-needed alternative?

Having learned that there's no point in condemning behavior without offering something better, a small group of Mennonite workers has opened an English-language school in the red-light district of Chiang Mai so that uneducated girls, desperate for work, can have a chance at a job with both dignity and decent wages.

On a hot June afternoon, girls from the Bible school bought buckets of long-stemmed roses at the flower market, and on each one they tied a small paper with information about the English classes. Then these girls, American and privileged, protected and provided for, went out in the streets and handed roses to bar girls, who would come running eagerly to grab one from their hands.

"We are the only ones who ask nothing from them," said my young friend Lydia, who lives in Chiang Mai and visits the bar district in her plain dresses and talks with the workers and takes them out for coffee. "Everyone else either is demanding something from them or is competing with them. I just try to be their friend. They tell me about their lives, and it breaks my heart because there's nothing I can do."

Jesus said that following Him essentially comes down to loving God and loving others. Not that this answers every cultural conundrum, but it serves as a foundational guide for life and service and sharing your faith.

A few years ago, Mae Wan, the laundry lady, rented the apartment above her shop to a young married couple who worked with the Bible school. They fixed it up and painted the walls and kept it clean, which made her very happy. Eventually she became something of an adopted grandma to them. They worked at learning the Thai language, and one day they explained to her about Jesus and their Christian faith. Mae Wan announced that she also wanted to believe in Jesus.

The morning we left Thailand, Steven and I walked down to Mae Wan's for our last batch of laundry. She settled the accounts and handed us our things, all wrinkle-free and neatly folded instead of on hangers, since she understood we'd be packing them in suitcases. She held first my hand and then Steven's and prayed a blessing over us, then hugged us both and sent us on our way as reluctantly as if we were her favorite customers ever.

"God bless you!" she said.

Now, back in Oregon, I smooth the T-shirts that Mae Wan pressed and folded, and the scent of her powerful detergent still lingers in the air.

I will never have all the answers to what it really means to follow Jesus and to relate to other cultures and to share my faith, but I know that you can never go wrong with love and kindness and enthusiastic service. I will never forget hauling that laundry home, stepping around the little lily ponds, and feeling the love of Jesus radiating from perfectly pressed dresses and athletic pants and sheets.

A Day in Prison

They don't allow hairpins in prison.

This was a problem. We Mennonite ladies with hair to our waists are used to winding our tresses into a bun every morning and stabbing it firmly with a half- dozen heavy-duty steel hairpins, purchased at the little Mennonite store in Halsey or special-ordered from Amish suppliers in the East.

But when we step out of our daily lives to help with a Freedom Rally in the alien world of a state prison, we need something different. We ask our modern daughters for advice, and they steer us capably toward spring-loaded plastic clips with curved fangs, plastic hairpins, and decorative skewers that poke in one side of a flipped-and-twisted bun and out the other.

We did our best, but we found our hair slipping lower and looser as the day wore on. At one point, my daughter Emily and I were over by the fence trying to discreetly help "Linda," who probably hadn't had her thick hair down in public a moment of her adult life. She was struggling with a beaded elastic-and-combs combination that was supposed to work but obviously didn't.

It was only one detail out of a hundred glaring reminders that this place was worlds away from our daily lives. We knew very well, though, that in this sort of world a minor inconvenience simply didn't matter.

A day in prison does that to you, clarifying quickly and precisely what matters and what does not.

An organization called Gospel Echoes, based in Indiana,

began a ministry to people in prison in 1976, presenting programs of preaching and songs and also offering Bible studies by mail.

A branch of Gospel Echoes opened in Oregon over twenty years ago and now serves prisons all over the Northwest.

About twelve years ago, Gospel Echoes held their first Freedom Rally, where they spent a day in prison and served a home-cooked meal of grilled hamburgers with all the trimmings to the inmates, accompanied by entertainment and lots of interaction with volunteers.

For years, Gospel Echoes Northwest tried to get permission to hold a Freedom Rally at an Oregon facility, and, finally, this year, permission was granted.

More than ninety people offered to help.

My friend Pauline, who normally bakes pies and bread for the Salem Saturday Market, baked and frosted six hundred whoopie pies, a traditional Amish treat made of two chocolate cookies sandwiching a creamy filling.

A Mennonite elder-care facility offered to buy the meat and shape hundreds of hamburger patties. They also provided the potato salad and many of the toppings, and volunteers sliced endless tomatoes and onions.

We assembled in Salem at the designated prison, where tall fences topped with spirals of barbed razor-wire surrounded a large athletic field and smaller areas close to the main building.

We waited in line to pass through security.

As Mennonites, we may be more accustomed to rules than most people, but not like this.

No hairpins, of course. No chewing gum. No blue-denim clothing (so as not to be confused with the inmates). No personal items except a driver's license for identification and medical items if necessary. Conservative clothing only. No cell phones, no sandals.

If we took a jacket inside, we'd have to wear it all day, we were instructed.

No delivering of messages to or from the inmates.

One by one we passed inspection and entered the "yard," an open area behind the main prison building, razor-fenced, of course, with the sparse grass of late summer.

In the morning chill we wandered around while the sound equipment was set up and tested.

Here were small, six-sided picnic tables with round stools, firmly set in concrete.

Over there was the "weight room," outdoors but under a canopy, with every bar and doughnut-shaped weight tethered to heavy chains.

Guards in gray uniforms wandered in and out, all of them polite and helpful.

The music began, and a small group of inmates listened, attentive, soaking it in.

A core group of Christian believers exists in every prison, we were told. Often, they face opposition and ridicule. A visit such as this from a Christian group encourages them to continue in their faith.

A large refrigerated truck backed through a gate and stopped on the other side of the fence, to the south. Scurrying volunteers unloaded boxes, trays, and tubs.

Men in aprons prepared the grills and laid down rows of hamburger patties and hot dogs. Smoke rose and drifted, uninhibited, over the high fences.

The morning wore on. Guitars played gospel songs, the sun shone, and men in blue denim drifted into the yard.

Finally, it was time to eat—the event everyone was waiting for.

We arranged tables into three long lines with plastic-gloved volunteers down one side of each. Large paper trays at the beginning. A hamburger and hot dog apiece. Lettuce, onions, tomatoes, relish, ketchup, mustard. A large serving of potato salad and a bag of chips. Lastly, a plastic-wrapped whoopie pie.

The men came in waves, fifty at a time, pouring out the doorway in a hungry line.

I stood on one side of the table, scattering sliced onions on burger after burger, noting the blinding contrast between our side of the tables and theirs.

On this side, starched, innocent, protected, upright citizens, whose worst encounters with law enforcement were speeding tickets and who were free to leave when the day was over.

On the other side, all men, all in blue, all ages, scars and tattoos in abundance, all with too much history in their eyes, and all knowing exactly how many days and months until they would be free.

And, yet, this was what we shared: the joy of a day in the sun, the smells from the grill, a plate of good food, music in the background, smiles and thank-yous and you're-very-welcomes.

They scattered around the yard, over four hundred men digging into, they said, the best meal they'd had all year.

We cleaned up and then mingled, striking up conversations.

These are real people, I realized, who came from "our" world and will return to it someday. This one has a job waiting for him on a fishing boat; that one went to Linn-Benton Community College last year and recalled seeing Emily on campus; those three love to barbecue and told me the best way to marinate steaks.

I saw young eyes that looked like those of my sons.

"I just don't make good choices when I'm home," a young man told me.

He seemed frightened, afraid of what he would do when he was released in a few weeks.

I gave him a motherly lecture on making one choice at a time and letting his choices accumulate into a new reality.

We are not so different. He may have to choose not to answer a phone call from a destructive friend or not to return to places he used to go. For all my sheltered life, I know the difficulty of choosing the right thing. The kind word over the retort, forgiveness over a grudge, even an apple over another whoopie pie. And I know how choices accumulate.

The singers sang of hope and forgiveness, of healing and repentance and starting over. The speaker invited people to come and pray for anything weighing heavy on their hearts.

"Me too," I thought, watching.

Who of us, inside or outside, in dreadlocks or a hair-pinned bun, does not need a steady supply of forgiveness and grace and new beginnings?

We left early in the afternoon, the sun still bright as we passed back through security; back through the gates in the high, shiny fence; back into cars that took us where we wanted to go.

We returned the borrowed plastic clamps and put up our hair the next morning with familiar, sturdy metal pins. In the following days, we cooked and cleaned and canned applesauce in Mason jars and phoned our adult children far away.

By all appearances, life was just as it had been before. But we knew, in some profound way, that we would never be the same. In the months ahead we would still see them, men in blue, eagerly coming down the line, eyes hungry for hope and hamburgers, with a smile cutting through all the high, wire fences that divided our lives from theirs.

Those Hearty Minnesotans

Minnesota is a good place to be from.

Granted, January in Minnesota can be a bit much after one has lived elsewhere for many years. You forget, for example, the startling burn of a winter wind on exposed cheeks and that prickly tickle as the inside of your nose frosts over at twenty below zero.

But there's no other place that offers quite that combination of a crisp, challenging winter and a warm summer that turns elm trees into the exact shade of green all respectable trees ought to be.

Even better than the climate are Minnesotans themselves: tough, hearty, and unpretentious; friendly and caring; and mostly Scandinavian or German, Lutheran or Catholic, with a few Amish in scattered pockets.

I go back to central Minnesota three times a year to visit my parents, who have lived there since 1972. Only one of my siblings remains there—my brother Marcus, who lives next door to Dad and Mom. I left when I was eighteen but have always, in a heart-deep sense, considered Minnesota "home."

But I hadn't been back in midwinter for a long time.

Nothing brings out the true flavor of the state and its people like a January cold snap. The week I visited, bitter winds whipped snow across the cornfields, and stubborn, slick ice made driving on gravel roads a nerve-testing adventure.

Yet I found, folks in Minnesota are oddly cheerful about winter.

My dad takes care of his animals twice a day no matter

what the weather is like. He came in from the barn on a Friday morning and removed his gloves, Russian-style hat with furry earflaps, insulated coat, and four-buckle overshoes. Then he marched over to me as I sat drinking tea at the counter and shouted triumphantly, "Twenty-two below zero!"

Dad is ninety-six years old.

Later that day, I drove him the eighteen miles to Litchfield for the annual evaluation of his and Mom's Medicare eligibility. I put two blankets in the back seat to keep us alive a few more minutes in case I slid off the road, then slowly lurched my way out to the main road in Dad's rumbling, old battle-ship of a car.

We stopped at the library. "Well, it's up to zero now!" I heard the librarian say cheerfully to a patron. I couldn't hear the reply, but then she admitted, "Yeah, fifteen below is kind of cold."

Yes. Kind of.

Below zero is cold, I would say, but below zero with a stiff wind is beyond describing with words.

However, this does not seem to bother my parents. Dad not only feeds the goats, the guineas, and his nine loyal cats twice a day but also fetches the mail at the end of the long lane and goes to church at least once a week. He buys and sells the occasional goat and is on the lookout for a newer car.

In the past year or two, Mom finally consented to a cleaning lady coming once a week. At age ninety-two, Mom sweeps the snow off the sidewalk before the cleaning lady gets there. She'd hate to see her slip and fall.

A nurse comes once a week as well, sent by Stearns County's social services. She came on the Tuesday of my visit and not only weighed Mom and Dad, encouraged them to eat more, and listened to their hearts, but treated me to that unique central Minnesota accent that you notice only when you live elsewhere and come back.

She reached for Mom's blue plastic case of pills, divided by days of the week, and shrieked in alarm. "What?! What is going on?"

Mom chuckled and pointed at me. "That's hers."

The nurse had picked up my blue plastic case—which was full of vitamins—instead of Mom's, which was supposed to be empty.

Relieved, the nurse laughed and said, "I thought, *Hasn't she been taking any of her medication? Uff-da!*"

I hadn't heard anyone say "uff-da" in conversation in years.

Maybe exclaiming uff-da now and then bestows a special magic to make light of subzero cold, and perhaps it's the personal care from these intrepid nurses that makes Stearns County residents live so long, placing them consistently near the top of the nation's longevity charts.

A *Chicago Tribune* article in 1998 said, "The women of Stearns County live longer than women in any other place in the United States."

The article went on: "Donna Walberg, executive director of the Central Minnesota Council on Aging, said community spirit in Stearns County makes sure elderly women are cared for . . . She has another theory on aging, however. 'Being frozen half the year, you live twice as long' . . . There might be something to that."

Minnesota is also a friendly place, where teenage boys strike up conversations with women my age.

I sat next to a nineteen-year-old on the airport shuttle during the hour-plus ride from St. Cloud to the Humphrey Terminal at the Minneapolis-St. Paul International Airport. He was headed to Phoenix, Arizona, to visit his dad. Just before the airport, we passed Fort Snelling National Cemetery with its hundreds of white headstones.

"Hey," said my seatmate. "Look at that. I wonder if those were, like, veterans."

I said I was quite sure they were.

He said, "I wonder which war they were from. Maybe the Cold War."

I looked at him. He was serious.

He went on, "The Cold War was fought here, you know, in Minnesota. At least part of it. So those might be from the Cold War."

I opened my mouth and then shut it again. We were only a minute or two from the airport, and there was no point in explaining.

Besides, who could blame a young person for assuming that the Cold War was fought in Minnesota? It made perfect sense.

I looked up the cemetery online. Yes, it was for veterans from a variety of conflicts, but the Cold War wasn't listed among them. And, even on an information page about a cemetery, the toughness of Minnesota seniors came up:

"Fort Snelling National Cemetery is the home of the first all-volunteer Memorial Rifle Squad in the National Cemetery Administration. The squad members are all veterans and each squad has a bugler who plays 'Taps.' As of July 2, 2010, they had rendered the final salute for 56,111 veterans. A special note of interest is that their average age is 71.6 years old and they have never missed a scheduled service during their existence because of inclement Minnesota weather."

At the airport, the shuttle driver lifted my suitcase over the slush at the curb and onto the sidewalk. "Thank you, Sister," he said, smiling. "You have yourself a nice flight."

"Sister?" Ah yes, this was Minnesota, where a Mennonite woman in a long skirt and wearing a black veil on her head is treated with deference everywhere she goes because people think she's a nun.

Inside the terminal, a woman in a wheelchair smiled warmly at me and said, "God bless you!"

At the ticket counter and through security, I was treated with gentle respect.

Then I returned to my current home in Oregon, where the grass was green and daffodil shoots pushed up from the flower beds and my husband and children were delighted to see me.

Oregon, I decided, is a great place to live. But Minnesota, to me, will always be a wonderful place to be from. I hope I never lose its best features—tough but friendly, pragmatic yet caring, facing icy winds with fortitude and a smile.

Motorbikes, Cobras, and Not Being in Control

In Oregon, Mennonite moms do not ride on the back of a motorbike speeding down a six-lane highway in busy traffic.

Also, Mennonite moms like to be in control of things, which is why it's good for them to travel to places like Thailand, where riding double on motorbikes is a perfectly normal way to get around.

If you try to look over the driver's shoulder to watch where you're going and warn her about that truck up ahead, you're actually far more likely to crash than if you sit back and enjoy the sensation of being utterly out of control.

For the second June in a row, my husband Paul and I, accompanied by two adult children and fourteen-year-old Jenny, flew to the city of Chiang Mai in northern Thailand, where Paul taught a three-week class at a Mennonite Bible school.

Since it was our second visit, I knew what to take. The kids, who each efficiently folded their belongings into one fifty-pound bag, accused me of over-packing.

I believe in being prepared, I told them, stuffing in medicines, snacks, pens, and magazines. Pop-Tarts for Paul, who likes processed poison for the occasional breakfast; a battery-powered fan for me; vitamins, trail mix, and a few more pens for good measure because I never feel quite safe without a good pen in my purse.

I was prepared for mosquito bites and migraines, for fevers

and food poisoning and flu, for blisters and boredom, for cuts and clearing customs. I had e-mail addresses for emergencies. I had papers, printouts, and passports.

As it turned out, the scoffers eventually came humbly to me for help with headaches and upset stomachs.

But even the most imaginative mom can't predict everything. You finally decide that if this is the place you're supposed to be, then someone will be there to help you when the unexpected happens.

It's as careful a balance as sitting on the back of that motorbike, braced yet flexible. Preparation must be countered with spontaneity, caution with being carefree, personal responsibility with trusting God and having fun.

In all my careful preparation, I never thought to prevent the series of events that led to the worst rash of my entire life.

At the end of May, all our scattered children came home for Steven's graduation, and we spent three days at the coast. One day we hiked up Cape Perpetua. I noticed a slight irritation on my neck as I marched uphill, but I ignored it, and hours later found a tick firmly attached.

My daughter removed it for me, and I was sure I was about to be deathly sick with either Lyme disease or Rocky Mountain spotted fever.

And we were leaving for Thailand in just a few days, where I had no clue how or where to get medical treatment.

Thankfully, my doctor saw on the Saturday before we left and prescribed a vigorous dose of an all-purpose antibiotic.

Relieved, I returned to packing, even attaching a little watch to my purse so I could faithfully take the medication every twelve hours, even through some twenty-four hours of travel over fourteen time zones.

We settled into our quarters in Thailand, switched to summer clothes and sandals in the muggy heat, and walked a quarter mile to e-mail our families back home.

My feet began to itch. Mosquito bites, I figured. More itching, with red spots up my legs. A friend hinted at bedbugs. Horrors. But Paul was unaffected.

Hour by hour, the spots spread until I was flaming from head to foot in fiery, red, swollen hives—miserable beyond all description.

Beyond a basic antihistamine and Tylenol, I was utterly unprepared. I couldn't call my doctor because we couldn't make international calls, and, even if we could have, it was the middle of Saturday night in Oregon. How could I explain the whole story to a Thai doctor who didn't speak English well?

Being sick in a foreign country strips you of any sense of control, which is at once terrifying but also strangely comforting because just when you feel most alone and helpless, quiet angels show up, giving comfort and support, doing what you cannot do for yourself.

The women's dean at the Bible school turned out to be a nurse, and we determined that the hives were a reaction to the antibiotic I was taking. Her quiet sympathy and advice kept me from panicking.

Mercifully, we reached Paul's doctor sister and my nurse sister by e-mail, and both replied promptly and agreed: Stop the medication and switch to doxycycline. Katelyn the nurse directed Paul down the street—"Look for a sign with a capital E and a backwards candy cane, the Thai word for pharmacy"—where he bought a packet of doxycycline, without a prescription, for one dollar.

My daughter Amy stayed with me when I was so loopy from the Benedryl® I thought I might pass out.

Small mercies accumulated. Our bedroom had air conditioning; Jenny posted a note on Facebook asking people to pray for me; Paul brought food; Steven brought cold drinks;

students offered sympathy and bought me an orange smoothie.

In a few days, the vicious red faded to pink, and at last I could delve into the experiences the culture offered.

We went out to eat at exotic restaurants, watched a light show on a lake, shopped in crowded fabric stores, took a ride at night through an exotic-animal "safari," and bought iced coffee and "cha yen" (a sweet rusty-colored iced tea) at neighborhood coffee stands operated by giggly teenagers.

Visiting a foreign country brings a constant nudging out of the safe and familiar and into the vaguely sinister. Cockroaches and monstrous spiders galloped across the kitchen floor, mosquitoes threatened us with dengue fever, and water from the faucet carried diseases.

One day we drove up to a lookout on a nearby mountain for an impromptu Sunday afternoon activity, hauling a basket with iced tea and cups and extra ice, all insulated in layers of bed sheets since we didn't have a cooler.

Steven noticed small tables along a trail farther down the jungly, overgrown mountainside and suggested we have our picnic there.

A small, elderly Thai man stopped us. He had found a snakeskin down there last week, he said in anxious, broken English, angling out his arms to show how big it was—ten feet, it looked to me.

"King cobra!" he said. "Maybe king cobra. In the grass."

My immediate instinct was to levitate in the air before taking off down the road for home at high speeds.

Not my family.

"OK," they said, nodding cheerfully. "Yes, yes. We'll stay out of the grass. We'll be careful."

And they smiled condescendingly and took off down the narrow trail.

The old man watched them go, thinking—I was sure—that they were crazy, but he had done all he could to save them.

I followed, gingerly, to a pretty but dusty gazebo, where I looked under every bench and up in the rafters before I sat down, eventually able to enjoy the company and the break from the city's stifling heat.

But we survived, hiking back up the mountain intact and with a new perspective on life: Any day you don't run into a king cobra is a pretty good day, after all.

My friend Delight, the delightful young secretary of the Bible school, offered to treat me to coffee at one of Chiang Mai's countless coffee shops.

Like women all over the city, Delight travels by motorbike. She clicked my helmet strap in place for me then I climbed onto the broiling, black seat behind her and we took off.

We passed trucks and zipped between cars and eased into large clusters of motorbikes at stoplights. I thought of how she could take this bike anywhere and there was nothing I could do, and of how this is not something I would think of doing back in Oregon, and of what great fun this was, cruising down Hang Dong Street, helpless and happy with the sun shining down and the hot wind whipping by.

The coffee and conversation were delicious, and Delight brought me safely back to our house.

Now I am home in Oregon, where the morning air is cool and misty as I make my daily list of things to do, trying to herd my busy life into a corral of order and control.

But I have not forgotten this truth from Thailand, that the sense of control is largely an illusion.

Scary things might lurk in the grass beside me, but I will have the most fun if I relax and enjoy the ride, trusting the driver. If this is where I'm supposed to be, then someone will always catch me if I fall.

5.

Reflecting:

Resting My Feet

A Knack for the Absurd

One Christmas Eve not so long ago, I slowly drove a car, with its emergency flashers blinking and a line of impatient vehicles behind, across Harrisburg's bridge over the Willamette River. I was following my husband, Paul, who was driving a forklift backward while a large, determined Canada goose kept up with us on the walkway beside me.

I seem to have a gift for moments like this, when normal life takes a sudden twist and completely random elements collide into a slightly bizarre scene.

My husband later seemed mystified by my sporadic giggles about it. After all, forklifts can break down on any day of the year, holiday or not, and the reason the forklift had to go to the repair guy on the other side of Harrisburg was that it would no longer go forward, only backward, and a car needed to follow him for safety's sake.

So it was all sane and logical.

Certainly.

And then I would once again think of that high-stepping goose keeping up with the forklift whining along in reverse and bubble over in silent giggles.

These sorts of things happen surprisingly often. Right in the middle of normal, an invisible curtain pulls aside, and I briefly step into an utterly absurd parallel dimension.

The pills, for instance. Last year I published a book, and recently a nice young woman from Ohio ordered a copy for her mother. I placed it in bubble wrap and then in a yellow envelope, as I've done a hundred times, addressed it carefully, and sent it off.

The envelope arrived at her house, she told me in a polite e-mail, containing not a book but prescription medicine. Two bottles of pills, specifically, simvastatin and levothyroxine.

Was I going crazy? I had never heard of either prescription in my life, much less taken them myself, and, I assume, neither had she. How on earth?

And, yet, there was her address, she assured me, and mine up in the corner. She did not help my self-esteem by saying, "My sister and I shrieked with laughter when we opened the package."

It appeared damaged and retaped, she said. All we could figure was that a shipment of packages had been run over and someone had desperately tried to match spilled cargo with likely-looking envelopes.

I sent another book, still feeling confused. Then, suddenly, it was funny, and I "shrieked with laughter" as well.

Only a day later, my daughter came in the door and announced that there were crop circles in the front yard. Really, she said. I followed her outside, and there were two perfect circles of dying grass, each about two feet across.

"Isn't this the point where people put on tinfoil helmets?" I asked.

Logic prevailed that evening in the teenage son's sheepish confession that he was "messing with the mower blades, to see how low they would go."

Do only a few of us have the gift, I wonder—some magnetism for the slightly strange? Or is it that these things happen to everyone but most of us don't have eyes to see?

Or—this seems to be the conclusion of more logical folks—do some of us take everyday life and construe it to be funny and quirky because we aren't content with normal?

I asked my niece Hillary about this. If attracting bizarre moments is indeed a gift, she possesses it more than anyone I know; beginning with the time she sat in a perfectly normal, hushed library and suddenly a clown in full costume burst in the door and shouted, "Does anyone have clean socks? I have a show in ten minutes, and I'm all out!"

Added Hillary: "And I was the only one who laughed."

She also had us in stitches in the retelling, perhaps proving the theory I've heard that stories happen to those who tell them.

Hillary recommends avoiding friends who sniff and say, "Oh, this is so lame," and, instead, choosing friends with a taste for the unusual, such as her friend Tiffany.

"She invited me to spend New Year's with her at a fancy ball, and made a special dress for me just for the occasion. It turned out to be at a ridiculously fancy hotel ballroom, and all of the attendants were very old and rich eccentrics with a great deal of nostalgia for the Victorian era. We somehow made it to an after party at the oldest, richest and most nostalgic man's house. There were old rugs on the floor, a pianoforte, and vintage muskets hanging on the wall. He served homemade mead and haggis."

Paul's Aunt Susie has never taken me to a ball, but she is always up for adventure, and I can thank her for a highly unusual experience last fall.

It began with a phone call from Susie. "Do you need bookshelves?"

Yes I did, actually.

That morning, out for coffee in Junction City, she had said hello as she walked past a middle-aged man.

The man approached her later. He was up from California, disposing of his deceased aunt's belongings. Could she use some household items?

They chatted. Susie mentioned her husband's health issues. The man had just the thing—an electric recliner made to rise and give an elderly person a boost up and out. It was almost brand-new, he said, and she could have it for the taking.

When she picked it up, he said he had lots more to dispose of. Susie thought of me. So she and I drove into Harrisburg in the van and found the house.

The man's name was Stan, as I recall. He was short, with a graying beard. He worked in the wine industry and thus had a different demeanor than the grass farmers I am used to. As we introduced ourselves, he suddenly looked at me and said seriously, "You know, you are just a beautiful woman. I just wanted to tell you that."

"Thank you," I said.

Poor Susie. He didn't say a word about her.

We went into the house. Stan took us down the cluttered hall to show us the bookshelves in a back bedroom.

He looked at me and said, "You know, you are just such a beautiful lady, I'm going to play you a song."

He reached past a limp curtain into a stuffed closet and pulled out a recorder, one of those plastic instruments that children sometimes use in music class. He looked at me with his California winemaker-in-touch-with-his-feelings eyes and played "Annie's Song," that sweet John Denver melody that makes you think of sad walks in a breezy meadow.

Then he put the recorder back in the closet. I said, "Thank you" again, and Susie just smiled. We examined the shelves, and his son and nephew hauled them out for us, and we left.

The only proper response was to laugh and relate the story later with careful imitation, because there was no making sense of such a bizarre episode, standing in the clutter of years and having a stranger play "Annie's Song."

Mostly, I have no idea why that recorder was right there,

within reach, just behind the old curtain. Also, we all know I have never gotten attention for my looks, not even as a young woman, and things have not improved since.

But, then, Susie said it turned out the recliner wasn't exactly brand-new either.

"Some people go to great lengths to keep the bizarre from happening," blogger Rhonda Strite said. "They create structure and develop rules and behaviors to effectively keep it at bay. They look good, (but) they are having no fun."

It may be a dangerous way to live, and maybe it's not for everyone, but I prefer the fun and suspense of knowing that at any time, in the middle of a perfectly ordinary day, random elements might collide before me in a quirky and unexplainable combination, creating a moment and a story as delightful and off-kilter as that determined Canada goose waddling above the Willamette on a bridge on a cold Christmas Eve.

Gifts Given Instead

There are gifts given, and gifts withheld, and gifts that are given instead. My goal, this Christmas, is to recognize and be grateful for all three.

The first are easy to see but often taken for granted—a warm, dry house in winter; a loving family; life and health; a job.

The second are obvious as well. We all know exactly what good things were withheld from us, having complained about, and wished for them, often.

And the third, the gifts given instead, we can only see when we somehow, against all logic, have the faith to be grateful for what was not given.

Late each November and on through December, our house and schedule fill with music. This year, eighteen-year-old Ben sings in three choirs; twelve-year-old Jenny practices for a piano recital and sings in yet another choir. All four still-at-home children will sing with their Sunday school classes on the Sunday evening before Christmas. Some of us will go caroling besides.

So "God Rest Ye Merry Gentlemen" plinks on the piano, over and over, pausing on the same suspenseful note in the middle of a line until I break the tension by singing the rest of it loudly from the kitchen. The "Hallelujah Chorus" wafts from upstairs early in the morning. Ben, at the piano, sings the same Latin phrase and hits the same keys a dozen times until he finally gets it right.

And then, time after time in this busy season, I sit in an audience and watch and listen as my starched and ready child sings or plays, and the music swirls around me in waves of unbelievable beauty and joy.

To be Mennonite is to be musical. All good Conservative Mennonites confidently sing one of four parts in a capella hymns during Sunday morning worship. They read the shaped notes and blow into the right hole in the little pitch pipe and learn to direct congregational singing with a pumping hand as steady and precise as a metronome. They lead four-year-olds in "Building Up the Temple" in Sunday school or reluctant fourteen-year-olds dressed in their dads' bathrobes in "We Three Kings" or "Hark, the Herald Angels Sing" at school Christmas programs.

In makeshift combinations, Mennonite families sing "Amazing Grace" and "Rock of Ages" at nursing homes on Sunday afternoons, while the elderly faithful bob their heads and smile and try to sing along. They pass around the old *Life Songs* hymnbooks at family gatherings and sing for an hour, the basses shifting into low gear in fun, old, up-tempo songs that no one sings at church any more. They go to winter Bible school and travel with the choir on a big bus. And they listen to Mennonite groups on tapes or CDs and analyze the altos.

Except when they don't.

There are not many of us unmusical Mennonites, but we do exist, and we learn to hide it well, like people who hide their illiteracy by "forgetting" their glasses and memorizing directions and phone numbers.

As incongruous, I suppose, as a Scottish person who can't stay on a budget or someone from the South not liking sweet tea, we nonsinging Mennonites often feel like we don't fit in.

We discover, far too young, that we can hear the music in our heads, but when we open our mouths a very different sound comes out.

We say "hmmm" a lot while trying to look intelligent, such as when a friend is rhapsodizing over the latest Esh Family recording—"It has harmony that gives you goose bumps!" We nod and say "hmmm" while thinking, "Oh, yes, harmony—that thing that some people hear when others are singing." When another friend is organizing an octet to sing at a funeral and asks whether we think Conrad or Jacob would be the better tenor we say, "Definitely Conrad," nodding sagely, while we think, "Conrad sings tenor?"

We avoid Sunday afternoon singing at the nursing home out of stark terror that we'll be the only soprano to show up. We get really good at silently mouthing the words to hymns when we sit beside an operatic singer in church, and we like to pretend those amazing sounds come from our mouths.

We think God could have done a better job of noticing that this was a gift we needed, being born into this community and all.

I remember when I first realized I had been denied the gift. Our little Amish school was practicing for the Christmas program when suddenly the teacher announced sternly, "Someone is singing too low." He glared at me, tiny and vulnerable in the front row, and said loudly, "Dorcas, I think it's you."

The horror of it. The shame.

Later came special forms of torture known as Summer Bible School programs, in which we sang rousing missionary songs about Greenland's icy mountains, after which someone would pull my sister aside and ask, "What exactly was Dorcas trying to sing up there?"

So music was the gift that everyone else got that was withheld from me. I didn't think this was fair of God, or nice of Him, at all. While I always insisted that, as a Christian, I trusted God with everything in my life, I never considered thanking Him for giving everyone else the gift of music and bypassing me.

But this year, for some reason, I feel compelled to give thanks for the gifts that weren't given, to trust in a purpose behind the withholding.

And I come to see I was given something else instead.

God gave me gifts in other areas, I admit. Sewing, for instance, which in a perverse way dulls my enjoyment of it. Forever analyzing, I notice the tiny tucks in the quilt blocks that shouldn't be there or the slightly crooked zipper in the dress. My daughter shows me her latest project, eager for praise, and I have to force myself to look beyond the obviously uneven seam and the too-large stitches.

I have an English-teacher eye for spelling and grammar, which means I can never fully enjoy a book or magazine unless the technicalities are perfect. Every unnecessary comma leaps off the page, every misspelling, every unfortunate choice of words.

But music, since I lack the gift, is wholehearted enjoyment, free from analysis and judgment and criticism. Imagine it— my children, up there in front, smoothly putting forth this heavenly sound. Flattened notes and uneven rhythms might be dropping all around me, but I am oblivious. They are amazing, and the music is beautiful; that's all I see and hear and know, and I absorb it with untainted joy.

The talented children—that's what I was given. The ability to sing well—that was denied. But when I trust the Giver enough to thank Him for what I didn't receive, I see and hear it clearly—the pure delight, the joy, and the glory of the gift I was given instead.

Trust, Suspicion, and Men on the Moon

The first moon landing, forty-five years ago last Sunday, must have been a very big deal because we actually found out about it.

Or, at least, my brother Fred did.

A lot of minor news slipped past us when we were Amish, since we didn't have a TV or radio, and we bought a newspaper only sporadically.

We five children shared a big bedroom upstairs in that old farmhouse in 1969, and that night Fred knelt by the tall, narrow window and gazed at the moon in the sky above the buggy shed.

Fred always gave you the feeling that he was in on something mysterious and astonishing. If you were really lucky, and really nice to him, he just might let you in on the secret.

"Yes," he said. "I think I see something."

We rushed to the window, my eight-year-old sister, Rebecca, and I, a year younger.

Fred was eleven. He knew everything. He said, "People landed on the moon today. I think . . . yes, I'm pretty sure I see little black dots moving around on the moon."

Really?

We leaned in and looked hard at that big, white moon. We squinted and focused and pretty soon we exclaimed that . . . Yes! There they were! We could see them too!

To this day, I don't know if he had fooled himself as thoroughly as he fooled us. Much later, disillusioned, we learned to be suspicious of anything Fred told us—after he had convinced me that the pig pellets in the feed room were good to snack on, Rebecca that he and she were actually twins, and my little sister Margaret that pennies smelled like pig manure.

It is comforting that everyone who knows Fred tells similar stories of believing the most improbable things, simply because he said it in such a way that you felt stupid and unkind if you didn't believe him.

He once worked on a dairy farm and pocketed a diseased tooth that a veterinarian pulled from a cow. Providentially, he had a wisdom tooth pulled soon after.

The owner's wife offered her sympathies when he returned to work after his dentist visit. Fred said, all seriously, "Would you like to see the tooth they pulled?" and held out the cow tooth, a vicious-looking specimen with curved roots two inches long.

He convinced the woman it had actually come from his mouth. He still has that mysterious magic that makes you want to believe everything he says.

I've found that the world is full of people like Fred. Not as charming, perhaps, but just as able to make you feel silly if you don't believe them.

To be informed on current issues to any degree is to be almost forced to form an opinion, so while I would like to walk the narrow path of reason and truth, I often find myself in one ditch or another—overly trusting and gullible, or unnecessarily skeptical and suspicious.

Health, medicine, science, finances, politics, parenting, religion, and many more examples—all have spokespeople who seem determined to persuade the rest of us to alter our lives to their theories. For every multi-degreed expert presenting his case as truth so obvious and verified you couldn't possibly believe otherwise, there's a counter-voice urging suspicion of experts with hidden agendas and guesses presented smoothly as fact.

Strangely, while the Amish are sometimes a bit too eager to believe the claims of alternative medicine and similar fields, many of them were skeptical about the moon landings. I lived with an elderly Amish bishop and his wife after high school, and Noah, with his deep preaching voice, would hold forth on the subject. "They say they put *de menscha* on the moon," he'd bellow, "but it was all made up."

He was confident that they had staged the scene to make the moonscape look real and then taken the pictures, even though he had never used a camera in his life and likely had little idea of how such things worked.

Perhaps it's because the Amish have been fighting the cultural current for centuries that I learned to be suspicious of other¬wise well-respected experts in science and government.

Or maybe it's my age, having seen experts proved wrong.

Bankers in the 1970s urged Midwestern farmers to take out enormous loans and buy equally enormous equipment. This was how modern farming was done, they said. Tragically, many of these farmers crashed and burned financially in the early 1980s.

When my friends and I were having babies, our doctors always told us that no, there was no way teething caused fevers.

But we were the ones up at night with fussy, feverish babies who recovered magically when their upper incisors popped through, plus we had a lot more babies than any of our doctors did. So we took their expert advice with a grain of salt and gave the counsel of experienced moms equal weight.

We learned about the four food groups in home economics in high school, and later the side of every cereal box told us that low-fat food was the way to be healthy. So we nibbled on pretzels for years, feeling tired and hungry, and then lost weight and felt healthier when we switched to steak and butter and steamed broccoli.

As a mom, minister's wife, and writer, I often think about influence and what it takes to change someone's mind. What makes us form a belief? What solidifies it? What makes us change it?

For many people, including myself, facts and logic are important but not as influential as experience, emotion, and relationships.

I "saw" the astronauts on the moon because I wanted so badly to be as sophisticated as my brother. Later, the humiliation of being fooled multiple times outweighed the satisfaction of being in on his schemes.

Today, I am slow to believe any of Fred's stories. I squint at him just as I squinted at the moon years ago, but now with careful analysis—true or not true? Hmmm.

This pains him deeply, he says, playing on my compassion with large, sad eyes. It worked when I was seven but fails to affect me now.

If emotions and experience make the difference, then, most of the time, nothing I say will change anyone's mind, so I seldom engage in debate.

As for convincing me, you don't win an argument with me by making me look stupid, even though that is disturbingly easy to do.

I have a burdensome ability to understand all sides of an issue and why people believe as they do, which makes me reluctant to push my point of view.

Most things are not worth arguing about, and in ten years many of the most outspoken among us will look really silly, time having proven them wrong. If you keep your opinions to yourself, you can quietly change your views as time goes on without having to endure the pain of publicly backtracking.

My faith is important to me, and, as a believer, I've been accused of ignoring the facts. I understand this viewpoint. Yet, the deep-down intangibles are even more real and true to me—conscience, forgiveness, hope. How do you debate such concepts?

My influence depends largely on how I make people feel, a discouraging concept for noisy debaters but comforting to people like me, who hate arguments but would love to turn everyone down the path of kindness and responsibility, simplicity and faith.

I will no doubt believe the wrong people for the wrong reasons at times, and then wise up and change my mind, as long as I live. And so will everyone around me.

What I want to remember is that we are all a lot like that little seven-year-old girl looking at the moon: persuaded more by emotions than facts, more by empathy than condescension, and more by experience than information.

Others will be influenced more by who we are than by anything wise and logical we might say.

The Gifts
They Ought to Want

I have a bad habit I hope to break before I die.

I'm reminded of it every time the children reminisce about gifts. Far too often, their memories follow a formula of "I wanted X, but Mom got me Y instead."

The cheap, knockoff eighteen-inch doll instead of the American Girl. The devotional book instead of the science kit. The shirt from Goodwill instead of Aeropostale.

I buy people things I think they ought to want, instead of things they actually want.

I have my reasons, of course, which I insert hesitantly into the conversation. Economy and good sense and Mom knowing what's best, which neither they nor I find very convincing.

The other day a young friend talked to me about the fact that for the first time she is in a relationship serious enough to warrant an exchange of gifts at Christmastime.

She said, "I always thought if I was going to buy a guy clothes, it would be from a cool store like Old Navy. But I was kind of startled to realize that if I was going to buy clothes for him that he'd like I'd probably have to go to Coastal Farms."

What a smart girl—already attuned to who he is rather than whom she wants him to be.

What did you get Dad for your first Christmas together?" my daughter Emily asked me.

I said, "I think I bought two different gifts and returned

them before I finally settled on a set of James Herriot books. I just loved James Herriot. And it turned out he didn't really like James Herriot all that well. He read the books but wasn't crazy about them."

Emily thought about this. "Wow, Mom, already way back then you were getting people gifts you thought they ought to want."

Maybe it's a mom thing. Recently, I talked to a woman who told me she clips my newspaper columns and sends them to her son in college. I thought but did not say, "Honey, you're just like me, giving people what you think they ought to like, and I'll bet your son appreciates those clippings about as much as my boys would."

In the back of my mind, though, is the little thought that maybe God did the same thing that I've done for so many holidays.

I don't think Jesus was exactly what people wanted for Christmas, either.

Everyone was waiting for Him, the Bible says, but they all wanted Him to fit their own wish list. Many wanted Him to free the country from political oppression. Some wanted a religious leader, obviously one that fit their own strict agenda. Most, I think, just wanted Him to satisfy all their wants and make everything all better.

Instead, He refused to get involved with politics and told them to keep paying tribute to Caesar, an obligation everyone hated. He told soldiers to be content with their wages and to "do violence to no man" (KJV). How was that supposed to work? He broke the rules. He hung out with the wrong crowd and called the pious people a bunch of snakes. He told people to love their enemies. He embarrassed his family.

What a disappointment.

Only a few caught on to who He really was and what He

could really do. Generally, the more sick, flawed, poor, old, and broken people were, the better the chances that Jesus was exactly what they wanted.

I have been on a personal spiritual journey to discover the real Jesus as the gift that I truly want.

Sometimes, even though I have claimed Christianity all my life, I am more like a Pharisee than I want to admit: more self-righteous, more convinced that I know what I need.

Last year, I woke up on Thanksgiving Day feeling as if I didn't have much to be thankful for.

What was God thinking, throwing this stuff at me from all directions—health issues, regrets, family stresses, and especially those private situations of silent suffering that go on and on but cannot be shared with more than one or two people in the universe?

Did I or did I not believe God had a purpose in all those things? I asked myself.

Well, technically, yes.

So why not be grateful for them?

OK, fine. I would try. And I forced myself to say the words.

To be thankful for the gift requires trust in the giver, which I didn't realize until I tried the gritty exercise of being verbally grateful for the things I didn't like.

This is what I have found in the year since then: We are all looking for something or someone one to fill the empty spaces and to heal the illness and to make everything all better and maybe even to send a bit of fire from heaven down on our enemies—not to destroy them, of course, just to singe their tails a bit.

Instead, God keeps offering us the same gift He did on the first Christmas. All the difficult things in our lives nudge—or shove—us in that direction.

Jesus still doesn't give us what we think we want—success,

revenge, constant happiness. Instead, He calls us to embrace love, forgiveness, and humility. Giving rather than taking. Contentment and vulnerability. Ignoring the noise to listen to the quiet. Admitting the poverty and brokenness of our souls. Reaching out to others to heal and be healed.

Slowly, we come to see that these are the gifts we really wanted, far more satisfying than the shallow items on our wish lists. We just didn't know it.

And, at long last, we say thank you.

Paul married me despite the James Herriot books. This year he went to Home Depot after Thanksgiving and used a gift card from last Christmas to buy some on-sale tools he needed. Then he came home and gave me the tools and said I can wrap them up and give them to him for Christmas.

We were both happy with this arrangement. It's nice, after twenty-eight years, to figure out what works.

I am more aware than ever that I am a mere mom and not God, so, this Christmas, I have tried to shop more carefully for gifts for our children, to listen harder, to ask more questions, to take notes, to get what people actually want.

If I fail, I hope my children can trust that there's love behind the gift and I want the best for them, always, flawed as my conclusions may be.

And I hope that in whatever life brings me in the coming year, I can sense the love of the giver, embrace the gift, and believe that this is what I really needed and even wanted, deep down, after all.

Second Chances and a Yellow Teapot

A unt Vina gave me a yellow teapot at my bridal shower. Back then, I was so ignorant of the ways of tea and teapots that I didn't appreciate this. In fact, I looked at it in confusion and sputtered something like, "Oh, a watering pot!"

Vina said kindly, "No, Dorcas. A teapot."

Oh! Yes, of course.

As I explained in my book *Tea and Trouble Brewing*, in the flippant imprudence of youth I sold the teapot at our garage sale before we moved to Canada two years after we got married. I still remember it sitting there on the table at our friends Joe and Nancy's garage on Brandywine Court in Woodburn, and I was worried that I was charging too much for it.

I look back now, shake my head, and think, *Dumb*.

Granted, we needed to downsize as we were moving out of the country with a baby, in a small pickup truck, and all our leftovers would be stored at Paul's parents' house.

But still, I could have tossed a few of the wedding decorations I kept for sentimental reasons and kept the teapot instead.

As the years passed, I came to love tea and to learn its mysterious ways. I began to collect tea things—china teacups, tea tins, varieties of tea, little spoons, and lovely, quirky teapots.

Then I painted my kitchen yellow.

At random moments, I would suddenly remember that yellow teapot and wish with a strange and wordless longing that I could return to the past and change my decision and keep it after all.

Of course, life was still good on a dozen fronts, and I was grateful. But that little regret remained. I always knew that in the grand scheme of things, regrets about a teapot ranked a long way behind regrets about words I should have said, friends I neglected, fears I listened to, and opportunities I missed.

Sometimes a small, tangible object becomes symbolic for bigger things of the spirit—easier to visualize and explain, less frightening to face.

This is the frustrating thing about regrets: They simply are. They appear at will, lurking on the edge of sleep, utterly changeless, oblivious to if-only's and why-didn't-I's and maybe-if's, impervious to wishes and tears.

I love the Easter season for many reasons, all the way from new dresses and spring flowers to the Resurrection and eternal life, but one of the best things about Easter is what it says to me about regrets and redemption.

According to the New Testament, Peter was the most impulsive of Jesus Christ's twelve disciples, quick to believe and quick to doubt. He talked too much and had inflated ideas of his own capabilities.

The Book of Mark relates the worst thing Peter did. Jesus tells the disciples of the danger He's in, and Peter promises, "Even if I have to die with you, I will never disown you." Then, when night comes and Jesus is arrested, Peter does exactly what he said he wouldn't. "I don't know this man you're talking about," he insists, panicking when questioned.

And then he goes off by himself and weeps in bitter disappointment and regret, and Jesus is crucified and buried.

Whenever I read the account, I think, *Peter, how could you?*

Yet, I know exactly how he could. Peter and I have a lot in common, and we are both good at regret.

But the story doesn't end with despair. The Resurrection follows, and, to everyone's surprise, their worst moment is transformed, miraculously, into life and joy.

Jesus seeks Peter out, forgives him, restores their relationship, and gives him an important job to do. His regrets were turned inside out, it seems, and his weakness turned to strength.

Recently, I got my own little taste of the Resurrection miracle in an innocent box.

On Peoria Road, between Harrisburg and Corvallis, my friend Loretta Birky runs the Country Bakery, where she sells delectable baked goods and also handcrafts and books.

A few weeks ago, Loretta let me know that she needed more of my books, so, after I volunteered at my children's school one morning, I stopped in at her bakery and we arranged a supply of books on a little shelf.

"Oh, by the way," Loretta said, "There's a box here for you. A lady stopped by and wondered if I ever see you. I said, 'Oh, every now and then.' So she left it here. She'd rather not mail it because it's glass."

She handed me the box. I thought, *Glass?* I was curious, of course, but not enough so to open it then and there.

I took it home and cut it open.

Underneath layers of packing paper, I caught a glimpse of yellow. I dug further, and there was a teapot. A perfect, beautiful, shiny, old, yellow teapot. Not identical to the one I sold so long ago, but definitely the same size, the same style, the same vintage, just a slightly deeper shade of yellow, trimmed in the same gold.

I was stunned. It felt like redemption and grace, like losses restored, and like magically going back in time and having a chance to undo a choice I regret.

Also in the box, since I evidently hadn't been blessed quite enough, was a box of Kenyan tea. And a letter.

Among other things, it said:

You don't know me (but) . . . I have read your books . . . you wrote an essay about tea and a yellow teapot you had received. You said it was unusual but you had given it away years ago. Now wishing you had kept it.

The next day or so after reading your story I went to an estate sale. There was a sweet, very old lady there sitting and watching her belongings go away. I felt sad looking at her. As I picked up the yellow teapot with a $2 price tag, she said, "Oh, won't you buy that? I've had it a very long time and it needs a good home." Then I thought of you and said to her, "I'll find a very special place for this!"

No thank you is necessary. Just "pay it forward" and use your new teapot!

This Easter season, my yellow kitchen features not only bright bouquets of spring flowers but also the yellow teapot, sitting in a prominent spot. It tells me that maybe regrets are not as immutable as I had thought, and redemption is more possible, and the surprise of Resurrection is still a gift for me to open and keep, today and always.

Off to Bible School

It's no easier sending the fifth child off to Bible school than it was the first, but just as necessary and right.

This time it was Steven, our youngest son, age nineteen, filling out the application for six weeks at Elnora Bible Institute and asking me whom to list as references. When Dad is not only the dad but also the pastor, principal, and employer, it's hard to find references. Also, it's a sign that his world needs to get bigger.

Steven and his friend Bryce decided to drive to Bible school in Steven's car. Oregon to Indiana, in winter. I said maybe 20 percent of what I thought of this idea.

"Call me!" I said, tearfully, hugging Steven goodbye.

"What for?" he said.

How do you answer that question? Preferably not like I did, with a pitiful, "Because . . . because you might get into an accident and die!"

"Wow, Mom, way to think positive. You always were the positive one." Then he laughed, hugged me with his big arms, picked up the box of snacks I had packed, and left.

They drove to Colorado and spent the night with Bryce's cousin Beth. Her husband, Cameron, sent me a reassuring message the next morning: "Your boy just left. He's clean and well fed, and, after coming over the pass, the worst of the winter driving should be behind them."

Steven sent a brief text when they arrived at Elnora. Then silence, but I knew enough about Bible school to know that that was OK, and he was entering some of the most intense weeks of his life.

It seems to be a uniquely Mennonite practice, sending young people off for a short term of study in winter, usually from three to six or maybe twelve weeks at a time.

The Old Order Amish don't provide schooling beyond the eighth grade. The more progressive Mennonites have colleges—Goshen, Eastern Mennonite, and Hesston. The wide, car-driving-but-still-plain Anabaptist spectrum in between has Bible schools around the country where up to one hundred young people gather at a time to learn and socialize and become established in the faith.

On their applications, these young people often say they want to come and study God's Word. The other reasons are more nebulous but still valid—to expand their world, to be an adult away from home for the first time, to make friends. And to establish what they believe, to find out where they belong, to affirm that living apart from the "world" is a valid choice, when so many voices say it's not.

These schools generally have names pulled from Scripture, some more obscure than others—Calvary, Maranatha, Sharon, Messiah, Bethel. But they go by acronyms—CBS, SMBI, MBS.

Steven is at EBI, an anomaly in that it's named for the little town of Elnora rather than a biblical reference.

When our oldest, Matt, went off to EBI at age nineteen, I expected his experience to be totally different from mine, way back in 1981, when I attended Calvary Bible School, a Beachy-Amish school in the hills of Arkansas.

It wasn't, despite cell phones and laptops and very different dress codes. As were Amy's a few years later, and then Emily's, and Ben's.

The intensity of it, the rules, the friendships, the opportunities, the learning—all were similar. And the awfulness of coming home, that was the same too.

All Mennonite Bible schools have rules—about clothes, curfews, Internet use, dating, and much more. In my day, the girls' dresses were measured when we first arrived. I stood with my arms out while a patient matron judged whether my dresses reached halfway between my knees and ankles or were too short. Too-tight trousers were in fashion, so the guys had to drop a small glass bottle down the waist of their pants and it had to clatter out at their feet unassisted.

By comparison, the rules at EBI are ridiculously lax, yet my children find them just as confounding. "No T-shirts in class? What's with that? How come we gotta dress up so much?"

Across the range of schools, there are unwritten rules about rules. Your school always has too many, and you laugh about them privately. But at least it's not like Messiah or Bethel, where your cousins go. It's understood that even the most straight-laced kids bend a rule or two. Calvary Bible School didn't allow caffeinated drinks, so I kept a stash of contraband NoDoz pills in my dresser drawer for emergencies. A well-behaved son of ours once climbed out a dorm window at night for some sort of remarkably tame adventure. But it's understood that you don't deliberately flout the rules all the time. Rebels are not cool or spiritual.

I'm told that the social dynamics are the same at Bible school as they ever were. For example, it's good to be "deep," the term used in ways seldom heard outside that little universe. "Deep" kids have intense discussions on apologetics and eschatology, and the "deep" guys are always called on to ask the blessing before meals. They pray the most impressive prayers of thanksgiving you ever heard as you are all standing in line before dinner. Also, they have the most amazing large, blue eyes with curly eyelashes, so, if you are anything like I was, you instantly fall in love with them there in the dinner line.

Later that evening, in the privacy of the prayer room, you make a deal with God that if you and Mr. Blue Eyes are both on for dishes in the morning, it will be a Sign. Sure enough, you are both on the list, and your faith and your heartbeat reach new heights, but then as he is spraying off dirty dishes at the sink he doesn't notice you at all but "accidentally" squirts water at the pretty and very shallow girl from Georgia with the cute accent and the little gold swirls on the side of her glasses. She shrieks, and they both laugh. Disgusted, you vow to be done with signs forever. That is also a rule, in its own way, and not found in any Bible school manual.

Dynamics in the dorm are just as intense, with heights and depths not experienced before. I found belonging there: In a candle-lit, late-night meeting we "shared our hearts" and were safe to talk about secrets and doubts never aired before but surprisingly universal. And not belonging: Loaning and borrowing dresses was a big deal in the CBS dorm, but no one ever wanted to borrow mine. Feeling superior: The girl in the next bed smelled bad and didn't shower enough. Feeling inferior: The Pennsylvania girls had "cool" down to an art form that I would never attain, with their chic little bolero jackets and big eyeglasses.

And, yes, Bible school also involves learning, both academics and things of the spirit—how to pray, how to believe, how to hear God's message to you in Scripture. Classes have a way of leading to opportunities. I had often thought of my life as a hallway full of closed, locked doors, but when Ervin Hershberger, the white-bearded principal and Christian Writing instructor, read my essay to the class and smiled, one door in that hallway opened and eventually led to many more, so many I couldn't explore them all.

Our son Ben's class in missions led to his teacher urging him to volunteer at a small mission in Ontario, which led to a year of cooking at a Native American restaurant in Toronto, assisting a small church, and big-city experiences a world away from sacking grass seed in Oregon.

Mennonites value community, and one of the best benefits of Bible school is the lifelong connections. Sometimes, your best dormie dates and marries your cousin from Ohio. You attend the wedding and meet not only all your Bible school friends but a man scouting for teachers for the church school. So you teach there for two years and marry a guy in the youth group.

Then, theoretically, thirty years later you meet the cool girl from Georgia who has had five children and is plump and warm and down-to-earth. You confess your past jealousy, and she admits that you always seemed so exotic because you had gone to a public high school. The deep guy with the blue eyes comes to preach at your revival meetings, but he is stuck in 1981, with thinning hair in the same feathered hairstyle parted in the middle, plus he has bad grammar that you never noticed back then, so you fervently thank God for not answering those prayers as you had hoped.

Bible school always ends, much to the disappointment and even despair of students. In 1981, I flew home from Arkansas and went back to my work as a teacher, high on a cloud of spiritual enlightenment.

Reality was not kind to me. Sermons were dull, hymns were slow, and the adults in my life could think only of insubstantial things like the price of farmland and picking up prescriptions and why wasn't Bertha in church on Sunday? I longed for the intensity of Bible school, of "sharing" what was "on my heart" with people who truly "got" me.

When the euphoria faded, I was still a better and wiser

person for having gone.

My children, bless their hearts, were exactly the same.

They came home and walked around in a distant, heightened reality, humming the new praise songs they'd learned and constantly on the phone with their new friends, the only people who understood them.

They acknowledged that Paul and I were saved, yes, but hinted much more: Wasn't it sad how we were so lukewarm and complacent, so absorbed in minor earthly details when God had so many heavenly things for us to grasp, so many opportunities to impact the world for Jesus? Then they eventually came back to earth with a new resolve to make a difference in it.

It stretches my imagination to think of Steven coming home in such a state, but Bible school accomplishes remarkable things. Whether or not he comes home on a spiritual high, perhaps even understanding why it's important to call his mom now and then, he will be a better man for having gone: his horizons wider, his faith deeper, his connections stronger, his determination to do good to others more solid than ever.

Seven Miles of Daffodils

Late every winter, just at the time when we dare to hope for spring, a row of daffodils appears along Highway 99E.

Across the wide ditch to the north as we leave Harrisburg, and then to the west as the road takes a turn toward Halsey, there they go—a long, thin line.

From Hayworth Seed to Fishers and their array of farm equipment, then on to Alford Cemetery in a steady progression.

On the other side of Powerline Road, they take off again, bobbing their sturdy yellow-and-white heads in the pouring rain, dozens of them, hundreds, thousands.

A pause for Cartney Drive then faithfully on to Lake Creek. And then, suddenly, they stop, a mile and a half short of Halsey, and the wide grassy ditch goes on without them.

Still in winter, we see dull-green shoots pushing up among the vivid grass. Determined buds appear, then the pop of yellow and white opening to the gray February skies.

Through rain and wind, cold and fog, year after year.

"He being dead, yet speaketh," the King James Bible says of the faithful Abel. And every spring, Bruce Witmer still speaks to us, not in any creepy sort of way, but quietly, persistently, through a thousand flowers.

"This is my legacy," he says. "What's yours?"

"There's planning and dreaming about doing, and then there's doing," the daffodils say to me as I drive by, windshield wipers swishing. "We are the difference between. See?"

Yes, I see.

I think of upstairs hallways yet to be painted, fabric purchased but not yet sewn, elderly relatives waiting for a visit.

"One by one," they say. "That's how we got here, by one task repeated a dozen times, a hundred, a thousand."

I think of books yet to be written, one word after another, each slotted into its place. Of quilts stitched a tiny triangle at a time. Of children slowly nurtured one breakfast at a time, one kind word, one little hand after another washed clean, innumerable times over.

Something in me wants the grand accomplishment, the sweeping once-and-done success, not the daily repetition of small things.

I never knew Bruce, but he must have been a master of the tiny task done faithfully, of beautiful results from careful craftsmanship.

He was a large man, I am told, a transplant from Pennsylvania Dutch country who never lost his accent.

Before retirement, he worked on a number of large buildings in the area and was proud of his work—especially, says Kenneth Birky, my brother-in-law and a fellow volunteer with Bruce at the Harrisburg Museum, of the Rubenstein's store in Eugene and its beautiful entrance. Unfortunately, says Kenneth, a woman in high heels slipped and twisted her ankle on the tiled floor that Bruce had designed so carefully, and, after that, his handiwork was covered with a carpet.

After retirement, Bruce worked on many projects, including detailed miniatures of well-known Oregon buildings, which are now on display at the Harrisburg Museum.

Like the daffodils, they also speak, of precise planning and then of doing, of hundreds of tiny pieces of wood, shaped and carefully put in place.

Bruce's wife died a few years before he did and was buried

at Alford Cemetery.

He drove out every morning to visit her grave, Kenneth says.

No one seemed to know what gave him the idea to plant all those daffodils, but I wonder if it was that daily trek to Alford.

Mike Lutz, a former Harrisburg resident, says, "I knew Bruce as Mr. Witmer. In the early 1960s, when I was about eleven or twelve, Bruce took over the leadership of probably twenty young hoodlums from around Harrisburg, as their Scoutmaster . . . after the prior leader left town with the money we had raised to purchase supplies for a one-hundred-mile hike."

"Bruce's legacy spreads wide in the area. He was a builder, craftsman, friend, and second father to many."

Mike adds, "In his 1998 letter, (Bruce) mentions that he planted three miles of daffodils from Harrisburg to Alford cemetery, to give it a beautiful view while driving that part of the road."

Bruce's yard was full of daffodils, I am told, and at first he dug up those bulbs to plant along Highway 99. Eventually he needed a lot more, so others donated theirs.

My mother-in-law, Anne, remembers digging bulbs out of the field by what is now our house and giving them to Bruce.

But he planted them all himself, Kenneth says.

I picture a large, aging man parking his car, getting out, gathering his bucket and trowel, crossing the ditch—down one side, up the other—squatting, digging, planting, moving forward another few inches.

Day after day.

How much easier it would have been to stay home and think about it, instead of tying his shoes, getting in the car, and going. Starting where yesterday's work stopped. Digging and planting.

Eventually, Bruce decided to plant daffodils all the way to Halsey, a small town nine miles from Harrisburg.

He did not live long enough to finish the task.

When he didn't show up to work at the museum one weekend, Museum President Iris Strutz called the police, who found him at home, alive but unconscious. After a hospital stay, he was cared for at a nursing home. He passed away in 1999.

Now, in early April, Bruce's daffodils have finished blooming for the year. The tall grass will soon obscure the last of those stiff, flat leaves, and then summer will come to turn them all dry and brown.

But I still hear them speaking, quiet and insistent.

There is thinking and dreaming and planning, they say. And then there is doing. Not once, but countless times over again.

And the doing is the only thing that persists, that speaks, that blooms every spring, that blesses the future with a row of beauty and faithfulness, seven miles long.

Happily Ever After

I think every story ought to turn out right in the end. The characters suffer, the plot twists, sharp obstacles rise in the path, but a good story works it all out beautifully by the final page.

Some of us read *Pride and Prejudice* at least once a year, just to make sure Elizabeth still ends up with Mr. Darcy. I reread Lucy Maud Montgomery's books when I'm sick with the flu, thrilled each time that Valancy really leaves her old life behind and acquires her blue castle for keeps.

I love to hear people's stories, leading family members to agree that I have a sign on my forehead: "Tell me the most intimate details of your life." It's fascinating, the invisible threads running through the life stories of everyday people, the strokes of luck, the miraculous connections, the accumulated wisdom.

I enjoy telling stories as well, especially to children, who for some reason prefer ones they've already heard. Trevin, my young nephew, has asked me dozens of times for the Chiclet story, a cautionary tale from my childhood in which I stole one of the pieces of gum my aunt sent my sister for her birthday. I was found out because Mom saw me surreptitiously chewing, and thus I learned that "the eyes of" both Mom and "the Lord are in every place, beholding the evil and the good" (KJV), and so I never stole again.

That's why people like me love the Christmas story. The world is dark, and God is silent, and then, suddenly, there are angels singing of good news and a poor, young virgin giving birth and "a thrill of hope, the weary world rejoices, for yonder breaks a new and glorious morn."

Something deep inside connects to a story, to characters and the forces that affect them, to despair turning to impossible hope, to the good guy showing up at last, and to a resolution that makes us close the book and smile and fall asleep.

We look at our own lives, with all our mistakes and frustrations, and we long for resolution for this story as well, for the loose ends to be tied into a neat bow and for meaning and purpose behind the strange turns in the plot.

I always thought everyone loved stories as much as I did, since even the most oblivious people in church perked up when the pastor's sermon switched from theory and theology to an illustration or story. At family gatherings, relatives of all ages gather around the storytellers, reliving Aunt Allene's suspense as the old seed truck with its worn-out fan belt growls up Interstate 5 and then—disaster—the belt snaps near Cottage Grove, and Allene climbs the fence and, despite many perils, finally makes it to Harrisburg with the load of seed.

Some time ago, when a generous benefactor offered to pay for me to take an online course in short-story writing from Stanford University's continuing studies department, I found that not everyone in the world likes stories as I had always defined them.

Happy to learn of dialogue, setting, and structure, I signed up, bought the textbooks, and started in. Most of the required reading was "collected short stories" by highly recommended authors.

I soon found that I had stepped into a sophisticated literary universe, where "stories" consisted of vague, dark, hopeless descriptions of people trapped in creepy situations. Nothing ever really happened, nothing changed, and while the words stopped after a while, the stories were never completed.

In the online discussions, the other students, mostly lawyers and scientists and such, discussed the stories' complexity and depth in ponderous detail, as though they actually qualified as good stories. Even a rural Mennonite mom doesn't like to appear naïve and unenlightened, so I used my considerable acting skills and contributed an occasional comment.

However, I soon saw the silliness of such pretensions and decided to be what and who I was, a lover of simple stories from the hearts of ordinary people. I learned what I could from the course and then happily left that alien world to itself.

Life had enough vague and dark qualities. A story, I decided, ought to provide an alternative where joy was good and love was real and every event eventually had meaning.

The Bible, while containing poetry and deep theology, is essentially a story, resonating with believers like me because we relate to its all-too-human characters and its assurance that mysterious and meaningful purposes lie behind every event of our lives. Maybe we're naïve, but in daily challenges and hard times of grief and pain, we reach for a community of faith that assures us of redemption for the past and hope for better things ahead.

"Think of what you were when you were called," writes Paul the apostle in First Corinthians. "Not many of you were wise by human standards; not many were influential; not many were of noble birth."

So Christmas comes, and simple people like me repeat the improbable story of long years of waiting and then a Roman census and a child born and angels announcing peace on earth.

Our children act it out in too-large bathrobes under dangling makeshift stars while we weep at its beauty and laugh with its joy. The story rings true in our hearts, and so we believe and find, not that seeing is believing, but that believing is seeing.

Then we cry some more because our own story includes many wrong turns and dilemmas, but here is forgiveness and peace, and we know we don't deserve the gift but there it is. We sing "Joy to the World" because we are full of hope that everything will come out right in the end, just like it ought to.